# CHOOSING
# DIVERSITY

Choosing Diversity: How Charter Schools Promote Diverse Learning
Models and Meet the Diverse Needs of Parents and Children
by Lance Izumi

January 2019

ISBN 978-1-934276-39-6

**Pacific Research Institute**
101 Montgomery Street, Suite 1300
San Francisco, CA 94104
Tel: 415-989-0833
Fax: 415-989-2411
www.pacificresearch.org

# CHOOSING DIVERSITY

How Charter Schools Promote Diverse Learning Models
and Meet the Diverse Needs of Parents and Children

## BY LANCE IZUMI

PACIFIC
RESEARCH
INSTITUTE

# Contents

# INTRODUCTION

"*In my experience, people think, 'Oh, all charter schools are the same.' Nope, they're not all the same. In fact, they're quite a bit different. But a lot of people don't know that. A classical charter school is far different than a STEM school. So, I think it's important to really make sure the reader understands that not all charter schools are the same.*

~ KELLY LICHTER
FOUNDER OF MASON
CLASSICAL ACADEMY

# Introduction

KELLY LICHTER'S OBSERVATION is absolutely true and illuminates the reason for this book. In the ongoing debate over regular public schools versus public charter schools, an important distinction between the two types of schools is often overlooked: while most regular public schools are cookie-cutter imitations of each other, there is a wide diversity of learning models used by charter schools.

Over the years, proponents of charter schools have offered many reasons for the establishment of these independent public schools. Always key among these various reasons has been the concept of choice for parents and students, plus the diversity of educational experiences promoted by that ability to choose.

For example, the California Charter School Association's definition of a charter school underscores the key elements of "unique educational experiences" and "choice":

> Charter schools are independent public schools with rigorous curriculum programs and unique educational approaches. In exchange for operational freedom and flexibility, charter schools are subject to higher levels of

accountability than traditional public schools. Charter schools, which are tuition-free and open to all students, offer quality and choice in the public education system.[1]

The landmark 1992 California legislation that established charter schools is among the oldest state charter school laws in the nation. It has influenced many subsequent charter school laws. Reading the California law, it is clear that choice and diversity of learning experiences is the *raison d'etre* of charter schools.

"Increase learning opportunities," "expanded learning experiences," "different and innovative teaching methods," and "expanded choices in the types of educational opportunities that are available" are all phrases that are used in the text of the law that underscore how essential choice and diversity are as the foundation for charter schools.[2]

Yet, the discussion of charter schools often treats charter schools as a group. As a result, studies of student achievement often compare charter schools as a group versus regular public schools as a group. However, whereas regular public schools are more likely to be similar to each other in terms of curricula and teaching methodologies, charter schools, by definition, are not only different from traditional public schools, but also differ from each other. Grouping charters together, therefore, fails to recognize the diversity among charters that is their inherent characteristic.

In my 2005 Pacific Research Institute book *Free to Learn*, I examined a number of individual charter schools in California and found that these schools used a variety of educational models to improve student learning and meet the needs of diverse student populations. Much has changed since *Free to Learn* was published more than a dozen years ago, both in the charter school world and, more generally, in how educational services are delivered. This book profiles charter schools that epitomize this evolution.

While test scores on annual standardized tests in the core subjects are still one consideration, other issues must also be examined as parents and students exercise their freedom to choose the right school and learning program.

Take, for instance, Stacey, Noe, and Edgar, who are elementary school students at Grimmway Academy charter school in the small rural town of Shafter in Kern County, California. Each of these students had safety issues at their previous regular public school, ranging from bullying to shootings. Their parents chose Grimmway Academy largely because the school offered a safer learning environment for their children. Their stories will be told in greater detail in the book.

For many parents, non-test-score issues, such as school safety, can trump test-score performance when it comes to choosing any school, including choosing a charter school. That is why the title of this book is *Choosing Diversity* rather than *Choosing by Test Scores*.

Education policy analysts are coming to this conclusion when they judge the school-choice decisions of parents. Lindsey Burke, director of the Center for Education Policy at the Heritage Foundation, points out: "...while researchers often look to test scores to determine school quality, parents do so to a far lesser extent. Parents prioritize school safety, while student performance on standardized tests is one of the least important factors parents cite."[3]

Doubt is now being cast on key aspects of current specific standardized tests being used by states to measure student performance.

The Smarter Balanced test, for instance, which is aligned to the Common Core national education standards and which is part of the testing program of more than a dozen states, including California, has been sharply criticized by experts. When it was initially rolled out in 2015, math education consultant Steve Rasmussen produced an analysis of the sample Smarter Balanced math questions and found that based on these questions the Smarter Balanced tests

"Violate the standards they are supposed to assess; cannot be adequately answered by students with the technology they are required to use; use confusing and hard-to-use interfaces; or are to be graded in such a way that incorrect answers are identified as correct and correct answers as incorrect."[4] Even more troubling, according to other experts, is the fact that it is impossible to determine if the problems cited by Rasmussen were corrected because the test's producers do not retire or release any items from past administrations, "so neither students nor parents can actually examine the nature of the test for themselves."[5]

In their 2018 critique of the Smarter Balanced test published by the Hoover Institution at Stanford University, Hoover research fellow and former U.S. assistant secretary of education Williamson Evers and former senior policy advisor at the U.S. Department of Education Ze'ev Wurman blasted the test and the state of California's implementation of the test on a variety of fronts:

> When the state adopts a brand new test that has not been validated against external known benchmarks...when the test shows inexplicable unnatural trends and the test-maker does not address them; when test results show strong bias against populations that already have academic challenges...when the state removes our ability to track the success of our students in multiple grades under the new test...then we clearly have a problem of trust, and we currently are flying blind.[6]

Respected experts say we cannot trust this standardized test to tell us if it is truly measuring student performance fairly and validly. Consequently, basing evaluations of charter schools, for example, on the scores of such a test would be misleading and would misinform parents and the public. Thus, the charter schools included in this book,

*Choosing Diversity*, includes both schools that have high test scores such as Success Academy in New York City, and also charter schools like Life Learning Academy, which has lower test scores, but which provides a safe environment and high graduation rates for students who the regular public schools cannot educate because of their extremely challenging backgrounds.

In the profile on Life Learning Academy, I feature Allan Pickens, an alumnus of the school, whose life, as we shall see, was turned around by Life Learning Academy and is now, ten years after he graduated, a success by all measures.

There are close to seven thousand charter schools in the United States enrolling more than three million students. More than one out of every twenty students in the country attends a charter school. Given the number and variety of charter schools across America, choosing the eleven charter schools to profile in this book was a subjective process based on my many years of experience in education policy analysis. That said, I believe that the charters in this book epitomize the diversity of charter schools across America.

Through interviews with students, teachers, and school leaders, plus on-site visits and the analysis of key documents, I was able to get an in-depth view of these charter schools, including their learning philosophies, teaching methods, curricula, goals, and indicators of success.

These schools are as different from each other as one could imagine, from geography to student populations to teaching methodologies to technology use to curricula. They exemplify the diversity that is at the heart of the charter school ideal, which is to meet the needs of each individual student.

# CHAPTER ONE
## Charters for Children with the Most Special Needs

"*I was always the kid that was picked on the most so that always made me defensive . . . Every day, just ready. Ready for something to pop off, right? Like everything, like every single day. And generally, I got my wish, like every single day something would pop off . . . Yeah, it's destroying myself. But I'm telling myself, I'm destroying other people. . .Then, I got my head on straight . . . you're gonna have to come back to Earth. And what better place than a school called Life Learning Academy that's going to teach you how to make it in the real world, because what you're doing now ain't gonna cut it.*

~ ALLAN PICKENS
LIFE LEARNING ACADEMY
ALUMNUS

# Charters for Children with the Most Special Needs

## LIFE LEARNING ACADEMY

ALLAN PICKENS'S LIFE was in a downward spiral. Not only had there been constant physical conflicts in his school life, violence was claiming those he knew. "The people in your life who are passing away because of either drugs or violence," he told me, they "literally would be there one day and gone."

"You know, I go to school, I'm fighting all day, I'm getting into it with people, I'm having all sorts of issues," he says. In response, he would eat out of depression: "I used to eat out house and home, like I would tear the refrigerator down by myself, though back then I didn't understand it."

"I'm a black man," he says, "so we have a lot of those ailments, the heart attacks, diabetes, stroke, things of that nature, but it had a mental effect." Pickens's weight ballooned: "Okay, 330 pounds would be a fair estimate."

Not only was his mental and physical health in crisis, he had stopped going to school. After three months out of his high school, he met with San Francisco school district staff, and one of them told him about the Life Learning Academy charter school.

One of the stock arguments made by opponents of charter schools is that charters cream higher performing students from the regular public school system, leaving lower achieving students for the regular public schools to educate. This claim is not only false on a macro level, it ignores the existence of charter schools, such as Life Learning Academy, that explicitly target the most difficult-to-educate students.

Many studies show that the "cream of the crop" argument is a myth. For example, a 2018 Arizona study found that the average student transferring from a regular public school to a charter school in 2015 performed below the state average on the state standardized exam in both math and English. In contrast, students transferring from charter schools to regular public schools were the higher performing students.[1]

If there is a charter school that truly busts the creaming myth it is Life Learning Academy (LLA). Located on Treasure Island in San Francisco Bay, LLA is housed in very humble facilities that from the outside are indistinguishable from the many abandoned buildings on the island, which had once served as a Naval Youth Center at a military base. Yet, within its walls, miracles are occurring.

Allan Pickens's story and background is typical of the students who attend LLA. As the school notes:

> Most students are involved in or at risk of involvement in the juvenile justice and child welfare systems. Many of LLA's new enrollees report histories of physical and substance abuse, and more than half have parents known to abuse drugs or alcohol. Nearly half report current or past gang affiliation, and the majority have profound histories of school failure and truancy.[2]

In other words, LLA is the last hope for these students.

The genesis of the school occurred in the mid-1990s when then-San Francisco Mayor Willie Brown hired the non-profit Delancey Street Foundation to assess the city's juvenile justice system and create a plan for reform. Out of this assessment process came recommendations for "an extended-day, structured, comprehensive school program that provided hands-on, project-based learning and school-to-career focus." The ideal program would have small class sizes and target young people "with a multiplicity of problems including documented school and family problems."[3]

Based on these recommendations, the Delancey Street Foundation developed LLA. Treasure Island, which is linked to San Francisco and Oakland by the Bay Bridge, was chosen as the site for the school because it was not part of any gang-affiliated territory in the San Francisco Bay Area.

The school opened in 1998, with a mission to create "a nonviolent community for students who have not been successful in traditional school settings." LLA welcomes students into "an 'extended family' which motivates everyone to give and receive support, develop responsibility and judgment, and build the academic, vocational, and social skills necessary to be successful."[4]

The force behind LLA is executive director Dr. Teri Delane. If there was anyone created perfectly to lead LLA it is Teri, as she is known to everyone. She understands her students because in her youth she was exactly like them.

When I sat down with her on a typically cold San Francisco summer day, she told me, "I never forget where I come from." She grew up in Las Vegas and "everyone in my family on both sides, all the way back, were addicts."

"At ten, I was already drinking," she said, and "at fourteen I had a needle in my arm—from fourteen to twenty I was shooting heroin." Kicked out of school in the ninth grade, her friends were her family, and like Allan Pickens, she saw many of them die. Of the four young friends with whom she grew up, "three of them all died before age twenty-one from heroin overdose."

"The last time I shot dope," she recalled, "I was in a gas station bathroom with two friends, I overdosed, and they thought I was dead." The friends left her, but "one of them had a conscience and said, 'What if she's not dead,' and called 911."

She woke up in the hospital and an older male friend was there and he told her, "We need to do something," and "I said, I don't know where it came from, I don't want to die." She was just twenty years old when she moved from Las Vegas to San Francisco, and into the care of the Delancey Street Foundation. "It was there that I learned about family," she said, "and it was there that I learned about community."

"I had to basically start from scratch," she said, "because I really didn't think there was anything wrong with meeting someone and cussing him out . . . so, I had to learn basic things that people take for granted that you're taught when you're a kid in your family."

In a miraculous turnaround, she got her life together, "I went back to school and I graduated, I got a couple of master's degrees, and I ended up getting a doctorate in clinical psychology." Most important for Teri, "It has always been my mission in life to give back what was given to me." "I always want people to understand," she emphasized, "that whatever your background, whatever has gone on in your life, if you get the right people in your life, you can change."

Teri says that LLA does well with three types of students: 1) hardcore criminal-justice kids but who have a level of maturity, 2) bullied kids who just drop out and are invisible, and 3) kids who just do not fit in well in a big school system.

Oddly enough, she observes, the hardcore kids protect the kids who have been bullied. The school has a strict non-violence policy, and "nobody bullies at this school, period." "We've never had a fight," she notes, "we've never had an act of violence at this school for twenty years," which is amazing considering a "majority of our students grow up in environments where they witness violence on the streets where they live and inside their homes."

Teri described one of her invisible kids. A friend of Teri's told her about a girl who had not been in school for three years. Teri went to the girl's house and "found this quiet, shy, beautiful, artistic young girl who just dropped out." The girl's mother was never at home so "she is basically by herself." Teri invited the girl to come to LLA:

> She came and that was six months ago, and she came every single day. Now she is only seventeen, so I'm keeping her in high school until she's twenty. What I'm going to do is get her a job during summertime. She's doing online courses and we're going to help her get her GED . . . So, every kid is different. They come at different levels and we'll meet them where they are.

All potential students have a one-on-one interview with Teri. She says, "I don't want anybody else's opinion in that room." "What happens," and she does not know why, "is that they open up and they tell me about what's going in their lives, in their homes."

A prospective student may open up, but that does not mean that Teri is automatically going to give them hugs—quite the opposite. She will give the students her unvarnished opinion of how they have lived their lives. Many students are shocked.

Allan Pickens, for example, recalls sitting down with Teri, "and I basically gave out my life story." "Now at that point in my life," he says, "I'm thinking, oh, here's this lady, she's going to, you know, pat me on the back and say okay."

"I give her this 45-minute sob story about how I'm the victim," he says, "and the first thing she says to me was, 'you're nasty.'"

Shocked, he remembers, "I'm looking around like, what are you talking about?" "I see your type," he remembers

Teri telling him, "you think everything is everybody else's fault, you don't take responsibility for the things that you do."

So, "like this woman I've never met before, who I told my life story, is literally telling me I'm full of it and that I need to change," said Allan. "And it was like, whoa, but she broke it down and told me what the school was about, if I work hard this can work."

The interview with Teri may have been shocking to Allan, but he had noticed that when he came to LLA for the interview, "no one's fighting, no one's cussing, no one's using drugs." He came away impressed thinking "this really is a community that promotes a non-violent drug-free environment."

Allan was not the only one who reacted to Teri's in-your-face honesty with amazement. Teri remembered a student named Tony whose father was a gang member "who really beat him up." His mother was married to another gang member. When Teri first went to Tony's house, she met him in the dining room. Tony had a cigarette hanging out of his mouth and a red rag—a gang symbol—hanging out of his pocket.

Years later, Tony recalled to Teri, "you came over and snapped the cigarette, threw it on the ground and pulled that red rag out and threw it on the ground, and you said, 'I don't know what the hell you think you are, but this is not what we're doing here.'" And Tony looked at Teri, and Tony said, "I just thought to myself, wow, no one has ever done that with me before—yeah, and I loved it."

Tony graduated from LLA, is married with children, has a job, and stays in touch with Teri. He tells her that he constantly uses what he learned at LLA to control the anger that he still has and teaches what he learned to his own children. LLA graduates like Tony have changed, says Teri, "because they never forget this environment, because it's not just about academics."

Much of school, however, even for a charter school like LLA, is about academics. Given that students at LLA come with so many challenges in their lives, the school employs special learning strategies to achieve its goal of "helping our students develop healthy, productive, and independent lives."[5]

LLA "teaches social, academic, and vocational skills, and instills self-identity, cultural awareness, and community values."

The school emphasizes individualized learning, which is not surprising given the many significant individual life and education challenges facing students. Each student "is assessed, supported, and nurtured to learn and grow at the ideal pace for his or her own development."[6] The school only enrolls up to sixty or so students, making it possible to implement individualized learning strategies. The teacher-to-student ratio is 1:6.

The reality, however, is stark: "Our students' prior high school experience is filled with significant episodes of disengagement, incarceration, and truancy leaving them with nearly insurmountable credit deficits and at serious risk of becoming high school dropouts," said Teri. To address this reality, LLA puts an emphasis on "core academic skill/content development and retaining engaging project-based learning opportunities and real-world vocational training programs." This combination, says LLA, has made the school "a local and national model for serving this population."[7]

In describing its project-based-learning strategy, LLA says that in groups and teams, our students work together on interdisciplinary, multi-cultural personally meaningful projects, into which different curricular areas overlap.[8]

Mathematics at LLA is a good example of project-based learning where different curricular areas overlap:

Life Learning students learn to appreciate the practicality and necessity of mathematics in their lives, through vocational and service projects. Students learn basic math skills necessary to balance a checkbook. They learn measurements through food preparation. They learn to represent and solve equations, as well as proportions, dimensions, and ratios through construction, photography, and engineering.

Science is also taught with a project-based emphasis. LLA says that hands-on activities and projects include: gardening to study plant growth, kite flying to study weather, using smells to study molecular structure, studying the physics of driving or riding a bicycle, using an indoor planetarium to study astronomy, and night time observing of celestial objects using a telescope.[9]

Students like Allan Pickens appreciate the project-based focus of LLA's learning program. Instruction is "very hands on," he said, and "you're not working from a workbook." Rather, "we're going out on a field trip, we're building things, you know, we're starting businesses."

Since students are often very behind in their educational development, LLA uses a method called spiral review, where skills that have been previously introduced and taught are reviewed throughout the school year. By reviewing and practicing previously encountered material, students are more likely to commit this information to their long-term memory.

For teachers, teaching students at LLA is challenging, but rewarding work.

Cassandra Blazer, LLA's director of policy and evaluation, first started at the school as a health teacher. In an interview, she told me, "you have to come up with ways to engage students using their propensity to talk to each other and be disruptive in general . . .You really have to use that urge [on the part of students] to facilitate learning."

In teaching health, she said, "I approached the class like a decision-making class." She taught her students to slow down and notice their thinking. In other words, "thinking about what you're thinking, and making decisions based on changing your thought patterns." Her discussions with her students were "always in the context of what outcome do you want to attain and what are the best decisions."

Craig Miller, LLA's chief operating officer, started as a history teacher at the school. He also used a strategy like Blazer's, recognizing that students "want to argue," and that incorporated "capitalizing and utilizing their desire to just blurt things out." Miller would give students some primary source material "that would get them angry, and then you would use that passion to then get them to look deeper into the material and understand why it was going on and what was happening in that moment in time and did it have anything to do with what they were going through."

He would also design his curriculum around Hollywood films like *The Patriot*, where students would take the role of a historian "and say, okay, let's figure out what's real and what's fake in this movie." "Teenagers always think people are playing tricks on them," he observed, so he would use that belief to get his students to think about and discuss why Hollywood told the story the way it did.

Besides core academic courses, all students at LLA participate in the school's job-readiness and career-exploration curriculum. The school points out that "our students lack the role models, networks, and other supports that connect other young people to the workforce" and, therefore, "know little of either the possibilities or realities of the world of work." To fill this void in students' lives, LLA has formal relationships with more than eighty employers that provide work experience for students.[10]

Among LLA's workforce development partners are the San Francisco Botanical Gardens, California Pacific Medical Center, and Yerena Farms. For their part, when students prove they can be professional and accountable, they are placed in vocational training and on-site internships, followed by engagement in offsite internships and paid employment.[11]

LLA, as a charter school, can be flexible with its schedule as opposed to the rigidity of regular public schools. Thus, the school may allow students to work one day a week and only require the student to be on LLA's campus three days a week.

LLA also has a strong concurrent enrollment program with Skyline Community College. Seniors can enroll in classes there, as LLA aligns its own start times to make it easier for students to take Skyline courses, and even provides a Lyft ride for students to make the forty mile trip to the college.

LLA's workforce development program greatly helped Allan Pickens. He described his LLA-connected internship at San Francisco's Cartoon Art Museum. Every Wednesday he would go to work at the museum, answering phones and taking admission. "It taught me a level of responsibility that I never understood," he said, "because up until that point, I never really worked."

Allan, who graduated from LLA in 2008, said that the school also taught him about entrepreneurship and starting a business. He said that he learned "what you want to do, how much capital you have to get to get it started, and really understanding business from the standpoint of a business owner." After graduating from LLA, Pickens eventually started his own insurance business. He now works for a company that services non-profit organizations.

Given that LLA students often enter with a knowledge base significantly below their grade level, there are going to be learning challenges. The school provides individualized attention such as tutoring to assist struggling students.

Teri says, "We do everything possible to help them catch up because, of course, they have to pass all the tests that everybody else has to pass in order to graduate high school . . . we take every kid that comes in here individually and figure out what their path needs to be."

"If they're struggling with school," says Teri, "we will try to help them figure it out." "We can tutor them, we can do whatever it takes."

The backgrounds of the students at LLA make student misbehavior a continuing concern. Teri says that suspension is truly a last resort. Instead, she will confront the student about the behavior issue in question:

> I look at somebody and he's high on marijuana and out of his mind. So, what's not going to happen is I'm not sending you home . . . Whenever [students] mess up, I'll come in there and say, no, let's go, you're going to help wash dishes, you're going to vacuum, and then you're going to sober up and then we're going to have a conversation about making the right choices for life, but I'm not suspending them.

### Challenges Outside the Classroom

One of the big problems that LLA is tackling is homelessness among many of its students. Teri says, "last semester we had two sisters that literally were homeless living on the streets with their mother in Oakland." Unfortunately, she says, "those two girls ended up dropping out of school because of it." In addition to kids living on the streets, Teri emphasizes that "there is a group of kids who have shelter, but do not have a home." These children may be sleeping on couches at the houses of friends or relatives, but they have no real home. She explains:

> What I need people to understand is that if you don't want kids to become homeless adults or kids who end up at eighteen in jail, and, ultimately, in prison, [we must recognize] the biggest at-

risk factors for youth to fall down has to do with strife in the family, domestic violence that they witness, and drug problems within the family. These are all things that are very prevalent, and so kids run away, families fall apart. So, they have to go live here. They have to go live there.

Craig Miller says that over the last several years the school has heard more and more stories from students "about not living under bridges, but weekly or nightly looking for places to sleep at night—sleeping on the floor, in a kitchen, sleeping in one room with five or six people."

Miller recalled one female LLA student who did not have a place to live and passed away from a burst appendix. "She didn't have anyone who responded appropriately," he said, so she died. Her death "was really painful for this community."

To address the homeless problem among its students and the problem of strife within the home that can overwhelm students, LLA is building dormitory facilities that will initially house twenty students on its campus. Once completed in early 2019, the dormitory will make LLA the only public school with on-campus living facilities in the State of California. Some skeptics told Teri that trying to build a dormitory was a "pipe dream." But she said she did not want a drug program or foster care or a group home. "I want a home where kids can wake up in the morning," she said, "feel safe, come out the door and into their school, and they can stay here as long as they need to."

This first dormitory, she says, "is the demonstration project." Her bigger vision "is to have a hundred-bed boarding academy, somewhat like Andover or Exeter, but for kids that won't have that opportunity." Teri believes that LLA's dormitory and the vision behind it will cause America's public schools "to stop saying, oh, what do we do about our homeless kids?"

The dormitory received initial funding from then-San Francisco mayor Ed Lee's office. After that, the school got a significant loan approved. Teri said that her husband, a retired San Francisco Fire Department captain, took $50,000 out of his own retirement for the project. "So, we have begged, we have borrowed, we are moving forward," she says, "and the city of San Francisco is going to be hard pressed not to love and support what we're doing . . . It's going to be a huge success."

LLA has been effective in significantly reducing student recidivism, incarceration, gang involvement, and substance abuse. Attending LLA improves students' orientation toward learning and increases their use of non-violent conflict resolution skills.[12] It is significant to note that although California has many high-performing charter schools based on state test scores, the California Charter School Association, which prides itself on pushing charter school accountability, named LLA as its Charter School of the Year several years ago.

Teri says that LLA has educated kids that would never have graduated had it not been for her school. "We have created a model for those kids that slip through the cracks," she notes. "Every single kid deserves any and all opportunity to have a high-quality education and a good life," she says.

"We're taking in kids who otherwise wouldn't be in school," says Miller, "so we're actually increasing enrollment, we're not creaming high performing kids."

Teri points out that around nine out of ten LLA students graduate and "a significant percentage of kids go on to higher education." In fact, according to Cassandra Blazer, 76 percent of LLA students go on to higher education, "which is an enormous feat for our kids."

Basic non-violence must be viewed as a success indicator given the environment where these kids live. Miller observed that "educators want to talk about curriculum and instruction and minutes and how you do there." For LLA, their non-violence strategy is critical to success.

LLA students agree that the school changes their lives. "I was the kid that was on my way to a bad road if I didn't find a way to change," says Allan Pickens. "I found a high school back in the day. Tough love. It taught me so much, so many things."

While he was a student, LLA sent him on a trip to the East Coast and he spoke on a panel at the University of Pennsylvania. He told his august audience about the different factors that contribute to LLA's success. "We were basically talking about how our school works and how our school is different from average high schools," recalled Pickens, including, "what we do to better our students, helping us to get a job, and getting into college, but at the same time, really getting into the mental makeup of a purpose—finding out what's the best way that we can get you to be the best that you can be and be productive."

Allan has kept up his ties to LLA after his graduation and in 2018 was named to the school's board of directors. "The best way to change your life is by helping others," says Teri Delane. "We have a stellar reputation because we are reaching those kids that no one else can reach."

## NYC AUTISM CHARTER SCHOOL

*I think the charter-school movement has pushed the envelope in terms of thinking outside the box in education. What you see when you look at autism education is the need for looking at the individual. Tailoring things in a way that . . . a general curriculum—a cookie-cutter approach—wouldn't allow for.*[13]

—Julie Fisher
Executive Director,
NYC Autism
Charter School

NYC Autism Charter School was founded in 2005 in East Harlem. A second campus opened in the South Bronx in 2017. The school was the brainchild of two mothers, Laura Slatkin and Ilene Lainer, who each had a son with autism.

"We wanted to work with the public system," said Lainer, "to change the way we're delivering public education to children with autism, to raise the bar." Lainer, who would eventually become NYC Autism's founding board president, explained, "We wanted high-quality services delivered in an environment where typically developing children are also found, not in a segregated school."[14]

Julie Fisher, who served as director of education before becoming the school's executive director, said that Slatkin and Lainer "were actually just looking to start a high-quality school for children with autism—something that they had a hard time finding for their sons in New York City." Then, "they happened upon the world of charter schools and realized that it was a very good match for a lot of reasons."[15]

The school's mission "is to provide individualized scientifically-based educational services to children with Autism Spectrum Disorder." NYC Autism's educational program "will promote the achievement of high educational standards and the full intellectual, social, physical and emotional potential of each student." Further, educational programming will extend "beyond the school's walls through organized outreach, training, consultation and support for students' families."[16]

In order to understand NYC Autism, its students, and its work, it is first necessary to understand Autism Spectrum Disorder. According to the National Institute of Mental Health (NIMH):

> Autism spectrum disorder (ASD) is a developmental disorder that affects communication and behavior. Although autism can be diagnosed at any age, it is said to be a "developmental disorder" because symptoms generally appear in the first two years of life.

According to the *Diagnostic and Statistical Manual of Mental Disorders (DSM-5)*, a guide created by the American Psychiatric Association used to diagnose mental disorders, people with ASD have:

- Difficulty with communication and interaction with other people
- Restricted interests and repetitive behaviors
- Symptoms that hurt the person's ability to function properly in school, work, and other areas of life.

Although individuals with ASD experience many challenges, notes the NIMH, they may also have many strengths. These strengths could include being able to learn things in detail and remember information for long periods of time; being strong visual and auditory learners; and excelling in math, science, music, or art.[17]

The number of individuals with ASD has greatly increased. The Centers for Disease Control (CDC) says that the number of children diagnosed with ASD is now one in fifty-nine.[18] Scientists still do not know the exact causes of ASD.[19]

NYC Autism provides students with ASD, all of whom are at risk for academic failure, with a comprehensive program of academic and support services based on the principles of applied behavior analysis (ABA).[20] Under the philosophy of ABA, "all people respond to their environment and, as a result, behavior can be affected in that environment." Thus, "the manipulation of antecedents (events occurring before behavior) and consequences (events occurring after behavior such as reinforcement) can produce behavior change and learning."[21] Students, therefore, can learn to engage in higher levels of pro-social behavior and lower levels of dangerous, socially inappropriate, or challenging behavior as a result of planned antecedent and consequent adjustments.[22]

NYC Autism emphasizes the use of small classroom environments and low staff-student ratios to promote intensive, individualized instruction designed to deal specifically with autism-related issues (e.g., excessive difficulties with attention or the need for numerous repeated learning opportunities to acquire skills). The school uses specialized teaching teams of certified special education teachers and other highly trained instructors to deliver personalized instruction to individual students.[23]

From the time a student enters NYC Autism, his/her skill set (strengths and deficits across all curricular domains), learning style, level of independence, and rate of acquisition is closely monitored through objective data collection and analysis. The school shares this ongoing analysis regularly with parents.[24]

The school maintains a 1:1 teacher-to-student ratio. For most students, however, the school points out that small group instruction will increase over time within the 1:1 classroom model in an effort to promote independence and allow for more practice of skills required for success in future settings. This shift is determined primarily by a student's ability to benefit from such instruction.[25]

Julie Fisher says, "We have the ability to instruct pretty much one-to-one," so "we have a lot of staff here for our students that allow us to do the high level of individualizing of everything that we do, which I think is so critical when you're educating kids with autism, because they're so different from one another."[26]

"You really have to construct things," she points out, "on an individual level." Parents, of course, are a huge part of the equation at NYC Autism. The school establishes a strong partnership with parents and provides a variety of initiatives and activities to meet the needs of students and their parents.

Families attend scheduled meetings with a designated family consultant. These meetings target skill areas upon which both family members and school personnel agree.

The family consultant offers assistance to families in identifying relevant goals to address in the home. Further, the consultant offers to teach family members or caregivers how to identify relevant goals, collect data, and implement teaching programs or behavior reductive procedures to increase skills and address challenging behavior with the home and community.[27]

"I sat in on a meeting [at NYC Autism]," said Robin Lake, director of the Center for Reinventing Public Education, "in which teachers and parents discussed data that showed how a child's disruptive incidents had decreased so dramatically that all agreed there was no need to track them anymore."[28] Lake reported, "The teacher used the rest of the time to ask how things were going at home, help the parents develop strategies to address issues, and think through ways to help with issues at school."[29]

## The Classroom Experience

While people think about a school day starting with the first bell, for children with ASD the first challenging activity is simply getting to school itself. Lake noted, "nearly all the students (their ages range from five to twenty-one) ride buses provided by the New York City Department of Education to school each day and walk independently to their classrooms."[30]

"That might not seem remarkable," she said, "but consider that most of these students are significantly verbally and cognitively impaired, and many deal with severe anxiety and frustration from trying to navigate a world that overwhelms and confounds them."[31] Further, Lake noted, "To help their students succeed each morning and afternoon, staff dot the stairwell and occasionally ride the buses to provide guardrails, for them, standing back as much as possible to encourage independence."[32]

Once at school, the challenging art of teaching and learning starts:

The youngest students are patiently taught to learn how to learn. For many of them, just sitting at a table and conversing with a teacher and other students is a goal that takes months to achieve. An intensive system of individualized goal setting, data collection, and intervention strategies is constantly being deployed, based on the Applied Behavior Analysis therapy methods developed by psychologists as a way to shift behaviors using positive incentives and reinforcements.[33]

"I watched a group of four young students," Lake said, "sit together learning about mammals and discussing one another's perspectives." Several months before, "none of them would sit in a group, and they spoke only about their own interests and thoughts."[34] What these students have been able to learn is a concept called perspectives taking.

Julie Fisher says that perspectives taking "is being able to kind of step into another person's shoes." She explains: Fisher recalled a student named Ralphie who had a difficult time understanding the concept of appropriate conversation. "And by appropriate," she said, "I mean really being able to check in with your listener and see when something you're saying is making that person uncomfortable or when they're bored of the topic."[35] In addition, "Being able to pick up shifts in conversation, so you can stay with what's being discussed." "Even joining appropriately," she points out, knowing "when you can add your comment in order to join in on something that's going on already." All these subtleties of perspectives taking were "very, very difficult for him."[36]

Fisher also says that teachers will "use a lot of motivational systems," such as token economies, where "kids are earning pennies or coins or points along the way." "And once they amass a certain number," she explains, "then they get to exchange that for something highly preferred."[37]

It cannot be emphasized enough how difficult and time-consuming it is to change ASD students' thinking processes and behavior. For example, one young student, said Lake, "couldn't tolerate anything or anyone touching his mouth and was suffering from significant dental hygiene problems." For months, teachers "worked with the boy to slowly, step by step, increase his tolerance for tooth-brushing and dental procedures."[38] When Lake visited the school, "the boy showed his father how he can independently brush all his teeth," with his reward being "a loud round of cheering and a scooter ride down the hall."[39]

Lake said that older students at NYC Autism East Harlem "have much more advanced goals and accomplishments." During her visit to the school, "students were doing simple research projects, simple literary text analyses, and all kinds of job-training tasks." The students may not be doing high-level academic tasks, but, said Lake, "there is also no doubt that they are working extremely hard every minute of the day toward clear life goals that their family and the school believe are achievable for them."[40]

*Politico* writer Eliza Shapiro said that in a classroom at NYC Autism's Bronx campus, she witnessed students working on math problems. One boy told her about an upcoming field trip to the Bronx Botanical Garden where he was looking forward to seeing the carnivorous Venus flytrap, his favorite plant. School officials told her that this student "may make enough social and academic progress this year to be integrated into some general education classes at South Bronx Classical Charter School, which shares a building with the Autism Charter."[41]

In another classroom, Shapiro witnessed, "A girl who has not demonstrated a grasp of language was at the other end of the room, playing a game called Seek-A-Boo to help her match symbols to activities, in order to develop a daily schedule."[42]

"Throughout the day," said Shapiro, "students filter out of their classrooms for a lesson at the school's weathered piano." She watched children match piano keys to letters or colors to build songs. "Every student has customized piano instruction, but three-note songs like 'Hot Cross Buns' are popular."[43]

Piano playing is not just an in-between-class amusement. One of the highlights of NYC Autism's entire school year is the annual holiday piano recital. "Many schools across the country," observed Julie Fisher, "have holiday concerts and recitals, but at the NYC Autism Charter School, the very idea of a holiday recital was revolutionary when our piano teacher, Eileen Buck, first proposed it a decade ago." Now, "it's one of the most important milestones of our school year, when students perform the songs they've learned in their weekly piano lessons."[44]

Students' piano instruction, notes Fisher, "is aligned with how we do everything at the NYC Autism Charter School: we work to provide individualized, evidence-based instruction to each of our students, allowing them to succeed academically and socially, and to achieve as much self-sufficiency as possible."

The advances that students make playing the piano is stunning.

Parent Linh Dinh said that when her nine-year-old son Toby first attended NYC Autism, she asked, "How could Toby ever sit and play the piano?" But, she beams, "there he is," and in each succeeding year, "he gets better and better."[45]

Eventually, it is hoped that students can be independent and be able to get a job. Navigating the work world, however, is difficult for people without ASD, and it is extremely challenging for people with autism.

"You know," says Julie Fisher, "the hardest part of a job that we're realizing more and more as we learn more about kids getting older are all the things around the actual job." For instance, "How you engage in whatever social interactions you need to engage in," or how one manages "the inevitable sudden changes or unpredictable things that may arise."[46]

Yet, despite these challenges, NYC Autism has been successful in placing students into the workplace. Robin Lake noted that the school "runs an extensive internship program in partnership with local businesses as wide-ranging as Facebook, Shake Shack, and White Castle." For their part, students "build resumes that they can show to prospective future employers."[47] Because of the nature of the population at NYC Autism, students do not take state exams. Fisher says that the school looks at each individual student: "So, on an individual basis we're looking at student achievement data—progress across everything that they're working on. As well as our own mechanisms for accountability in terms of parent participation, all the other charter objectives that we have to adhere to."[48]

Parents have voted with their feet and have jammed the doors of NYC Autism. The school's East Harlem and South Bronx campuses serve a combined total of more than forty students. In 2017, the East Harlem campus had a waiting list of 108 families for three open spots.[49]

Students are categorized by the level of severity of their ASD, and lotteries for spaces are done for each of those categories.

The taxpayer's cost per pupil is in the $80,000 per year range, but experts say that this cost is lower than paying for students with the most serious needs to attend private schools. Catherine Lord, director of the Center for Autism and the Developing Brain at Weill Cornell Medicine/New York-Presbyterian, observed, "The more of these schools that could exist in a public school setting, the more the taxpayer would save." Due to the success that NYC Autism has with its students, she believes that the school's students will need fewer public services, including hospital visits, later in life.[50]

Parents express great satisfaction with the outcomes that NYC Autism produces for their children. Robin Lake noted, "what this school is doing for their parents is life-changing." As an example, she described the experience of one family:

> One young student's mother had not been able to attend church since he was a baby because he was disruptive during the service. After intensive therapy at school, the family recently began attending church together again. The father I met was glowing when he spoke about how proud he is of his son's progress and how much better things are at home now that they have strategies that work.[51]

Eliza Shapiro noted that NYC Autism has won praise from experts on all sides of the charter-school debate, and "demonstrates how children with the most severe needs can be educated in a public setting, rather than in the private schools where many affluent parents manage to send their children with disabilities."[52]

New York City Council Speaker Melissa Mark-Viverito, a sometime critic of charter schools, takes a more favorable view of NYC Autism Charter School. "All students—especially the most vulnerable—deserve access to quality education," she commented, "and the New York City Autism Charter has been a welcome addition to the El Barrio/East Harlem neighborhood."[53]

Speaking to the equity issue, Julie Fisher says that many NYC Autism students "come from the local neighborhood" and "wouldn't typically be able to access a private school program or this level of education."[54] Eliza Shapiro observed that NYC Autism "could only exist as a charter, outside the bureaucratic strictures of traditional public schools where teachers are free to adapt to a child's specific needs in real time."[55]

"Many people see limitations when they imagine children on the Autism Spectrum," says Julie Fisher. "When individuals with autism have the right support," which she and her colleagues at NYC Autism provide, "they can accomplish amazing things, and develop skills that will last a lifetime."[56]

# CHAPTER TWO
## Diversity Within Diversity

" *If we teach today's students as we taught yesterday's, we rob them of tomorrow.*

~ JOHN DEWEY
AMERICAN EDUCATION
REFORMER

# Diversity Within Diversity

## NATOMAS CHARTER SCHOOL

"MOST CHARTER SCHOOLS," says Natomas Charter School co-founder and executive director Ting Sun, "have this one way of doing things." At her school, there are "very different things all happening under one roof." Welcome to Natomas Charter School, which by itself may best epitomize the title of this book—Choosing Diversity.

Natomas Charter School, which is in the suburban Natomas area of Sacramento, California, has five very different individual academies operating under its umbrella: the Leading Edge Academy, the Performing and Fine Arts Academy, the Pursuing Academic Choices Together Academy, the Star Academy, and the Virtual Learning Academy.

Ting Sun was appointed to the California State Board of Education in 2015 by Governor Jerry Brown. She is an education reformer who exudes commitment and energy. Our conversation began with her favorite quote from John Dewey: 'If we teach today's students as we taught yesterday's, we rob them of tomorrow.'"

She credits her co-founder and husband Charlie Leo with the vision that created their five-academy model:

He always said that he looked at our academies as spokes on a wheel. And we're trying to create a wheel where every kid belongs. And so, we've created these different spokes, so to attract different kinds of students, and we purposely develop folks in those academics that are different than what is currently in the traditional system.

Natomas Charter School is one of California's charter school pioneers. When California passed its landmark charter school law in the early 1990s, Natomas Charter School was one of the first charters to be established. "When the idea of charters came into law," recalled Sun, "the science teacher at the middle school where I was teaching and I decided that we needed to do something different with middle schoolers."

"We had all these ideas around curriculum and to do more hands-on activities, and we wanted more parental involvement, technology, all these things," she explained, "and we were kind of griping about it in our teachers lunch room." And like Saint Paul on his way to Damascus, Sun and her colleague had an epiphany, "and then the idea of chartering came about and we decided to put our money where our mouth was and put some work into it and design our own school. . . .We were just teachers who wanted to do something a little different and the chartering concept came in and gave the opportunity to do that." Sun continued, "We really just wanted an opportunity to be able to take things we were doing in our classrooms and expand them." As she looks back, "it was just this concept, this opportunity we couldn't pass up."

Armed with the enthusiasm of a new idea, Sun and Leo went recruiting for parents and their children. "We basically went out there and just did community meetings,"

Sun remembered. "We started talking to parents about what our ideas were and we got parents to actually buy into the concept and got students to buy into the concept."

She and Charlie Leo stressed "the experiential learning aspect of things, and that we were really trying to be progressive and thinking about 21st century learning at a time when we were still in the 20th century."

"We wanted to try to motivate kids at that middle-school level to stretch and be lifelong learners," she said, and "become invested in their own education . . . .The only way to do that is to tap into their interests and what they wanted to do and were interested in doing."

## Experiential and Lifelong Learning

Sun said that students who come to the different five academies are interested in a specific area or because there is something about the structure that resonates with them. For students, she says, the academies are "unique niches."

Established in 1993, the Leading Edge Academy was the school's first academy, followed in 1994 by the school's homeschooling academy, Pursuing Academic Choice Together, the Performing and Fine Arts Academy in 1997, the Virtual Learning Academy in 2000, and the Star Academy in 2010-11.

The school has grown from eighty students its first year to more than one thousand eight hundred today.

Many in Sacramento know the school best for its Performing and Fine Arts Academy (PFAA) and professional quality stage productions. I attended a performance of the musical *Hairspray* at Natomas Charter School a few years ago. I expected a typical high school production—earnest, but not much more than that. Was I wrong. I was struck by the amazing level of performance of not only the lead performers, but of all the student cast members.

PFAA, which is a middle and high school classroom-based program for grades six through twelve, emphasizes college preparatory, core academics, while offering intensive artistic training through a broad range of elective courses. Available art disciplines range from drama, dance, music and the fine arts to stagecraft and digital arts and are taught by professional artists.[1]

Receiving instruction from professional practicing artists, says the school, allows students to learn the technical aspects of artistic expression and to gather a deeper understanding of the career of a professional practicing artist.[2]

PFAA's mission statement says that the academy is dedicated to preparing "students with strong personal interests in the arts to successfully pursue entry into an institute of higher learning and/or a career in the performing and fine arts by channeling their unique skills and talents through an intense, integrated academic and arts program which focuses on a whole-person development approach to learning in unity with high academic and artistic standards."[3]

The school notes that as a result of their passion, academic commitment, and artistic training, over 70 percent of PFAA students consistently make the honor roll, and over 96 percent of high school seniors who apply go on to prestigious four-year universities and art schools.[4]

Natomas Charter School uses a lottery system to admit students on a random basis. The only academy that has an additional admissions process is PFAA, which requires an audition.

At PFAA, the four core areas are drama and theater, dance, visual arts and music. Within those core areas there are sub-areas, such as technical theater and acting within drama and jazz, ballet, modern, and tap within dance.

Sun noted, "The philosophy of PFAA is that academics and art sit on the same level, not one is above the other." There is a balance between academic courses that meet the requirements of the University of California and the California State University, plus "we also have on the art side a selected arts pathway so students graduate with distinction in one of the arts areas and they also get [college-prep courses]."

What about the student experience at the Performing and Fine Arts Academy? Allie is a 2018 graduate of PFAA at Natomas Charter School.

Allie said that she remembered having to go to PFAA for auditions as an entering middle schooler: "Basically, we went to four different art forms." For instance, in drawing, she had to redraw something upside down. She had to do some dance performance. But, as Sun said, the process was not stressful, and Allie had to answer a few questions by interviewers, and then waited to hear back. She recalled "getting the acceptance letter and I was so excited."

She gravitated toward visual arts "because it's something I love." With the enthusiasm of a young person discovering herself, she took a painting class saying, "I remember just how much I love painting." "I was able to develop my skill and I was able to get better." She came to an emotional place "where I was just like, this is relaxing."

Allie said that her painting class "forced me to just jump in and do it, try new things, learn new techniques." Specifically, she recalled:

> I tried techniques that I'd never even thought of before. So, the curriculum included things like cubism and different styles of painting, like pop art. And I've never painted in those styles before, but when I did, it opened me up and made me learn new techniques that I had no idea of before, but you ended up being able to do them very well.

Her favorite painting style turned out to be pop art: "I'm like Andy Warhol, yeah. Roy Lichtenstein, yeah. I love that comic book style."

Recall that Ting Sun said that one of the key reasons she and Charlie Leo founded Natomas Charter School was to offer experiential learning. Allie validated that the school had met that goal:

> There's not a lot of textbooks. There's a lot of learning from experience. And I think that's important because visual, you know, if you're always learning from textbooks, why?

The capstone for PFAA students is the senior project. Allie's senior project, a beautiful painted mural, which Ting Sun showed me when I visited the school, adorns the interior of the counseling office.

One of the counselors gave her the idea of doing a mural for her new room, and she got the idea for the subject of the mural—a colorful peaceful ocean scene of sea turtles, fish, jellyfish, whales and anemones—by talking to the counseling staff: "What do you see for this room? What kind of art do you want? What do you think is the mood?" "I just wanted to produce something that ultimately was for them."

In a musical production such as "Hairspray," Allie said, "multiple senior projects went behind that show." "Running the tech of the show could be a senior project, doing all the costumes or organizing make up, or making the score for shows could be senior projects."

While she was taking the various arts classes, Allie was also taking regular core subject classes as well. For example, her English classes gave her "the opportunity to explore my writing . . . and I was able to find my style of writing as well."

So, what was the end result of all these experiences? For Allie, she became a "totally different person," with "understanding and appreciation for different things." She had to overcome many challenges while at PFAA:

There was a point in time where it was really challenging for me . . . but I am really glad I was able to stick with it and get through because I learned so much and I love the classes I took and I love the person I've come to be. I really think I've developed skills and understanding for a lot of things, and I don't think I would have been able to do that without being encouraged.

Allie thinks that the difference between a regular public school and a charter school is that in charter schools, each student is different and that charter schools like Natomas Charter School are able to address those individual needs: "I think a lot of people wanted to get that 'real' high school experience. But I think everyone is unique. And I think when you go to a charter you really get a unique high school experience.

Allie, who has started as a freshman at California State University Sacramento, says that her experience at PFAA has really prepared her for college-level work. She took a summer English course at CSUS and said, "the course load is a lot of work, but compared to charter it's the same level." In contrast, "I think a lot of kids from a traditional public high school are shocked" with the "amount and difficulty of the work."

While some PFAA graduates do go on to careers in the arts, others make use of their arts education in their non-arts studies and jobs. As Allie's experience emphasizes, the unique education she received at Natomas Charter School will impact her throughout her entire life.

Among the other academies, the Leading Edge Academy (LE), the school's first academy, is a middle school that has a cross-curricular three-year program that involves students in hands-on learning experiences and encourages creativity and exploration. The school says that LE is based on five pillars: building leadership, creative problem solving, technical savvy, appreciating cultural diversity, and global thinking. LE offers students "a collaborative, project-based and technology-focused setting."

The evolution of technology has been an important factor in the evolution of the academy. According to Ting Sun:

> What used to be our computer lab no longer has any computers in it. It just has iPads. And it's become an innovation lab where students can do engineering-type things. So, they have robotics and they have other types of tools that they can utilize to create projects. And so, it's not just about getting on the computer anymore, because we're way beyond that. It's about how you utilize different types of technology to express your understanding of things, to create new things and new projects, to test out concepts.

LE seeks to integrate technology across subject fields, rather than keeping it in a silo as often happens in many public schools. "So, students might," Sun observed, "look at a world-wide issue or they may look at a school-wide issue and then figure out ways to solve or resolve those issues using science." The technology solutions involve advocating, communicating, and writing so that the projects are integrated and connect all those areas together.

The Pursuing Academic Choices Together (PACT) has fewer than two hundred students serving parents who homeschool their children in eight counties in the Sacramento region.

In PACT, parents instruct their children at home under the guidance of a certificated homeschool adviser and by teachers in a classroom setting.

In addition to their home schooling, PACT students attend enrichment classes at the school's PACT campus. These classes include dance, music, choir, drama, hands-on art, computers, coding, social thinking and science classes.

On-campus classes are all taught by credentialed educators. Amazingly, PACT offers more than seventy enrichment courses for students in mixed-age groups.[5]

PACT also runs a small hybrid program called Project X for seventh and eighth grade students. In Project X, students attend classes on the PACT campus two days a week and participate in an online learning program three days a week.[6]

Ting Sun says that, "the basic tenet of our philosophy is that we wrap the education around the child. We don't try to get the child to bend to the education. So, PACT is the essence of that 'around the child' philosophy."

PACT, Sun says, is not only for those parents who already homeschool their children. It is also for parents who have not thought of homeschooling but has a child with special needs or needs an individualized program. These parents come to PACT and they are provided with a multitude of curricula from which to choose.

The teacher advisors are usually veteran teachers who have worked with many different students. Sun says that they really know the curricula and can help support the parent.

The school's Virtual Learning Academy (VLA), like its homeschool sister academy, is a kind of hybrid, too. It is a high school for students in grades nine through twelve and serves students who need a flexible schedule to do their best work and learning.

VLA attracts a wide variety of students who are in different situations. Sun says that the academy gets accelerated students who want to just graduate in three years, and students who are also behind on credits.

VLA students, says the school, "takes advantage of the flexibility provided by an online classroom to complete modules, participate in online discussion, and complete and submit online assignments when it fits into their daily schedule."[7]

VLA does not use a curriculum package that is the product of outside developers. Rather, VLA teachers design the curriculum. Sun says, "The activities, the assignments, the tests are all designed by our teachers internally, and they are constantly updating them," and then posting them in an online platform with full access to the VLA's students.

The independent study online assignments are enhanced with weekly classroom-based workshops. While in these classes, students complete wet labs, participate in Socratic discussions, work with small groups, and engage in hands-on learning experiences.[8]

Sun says that what makes virtual learning different at VLA is that "we do have that part where there's the accountability through our workshops that gives our teachers a way to monitor students as they move along, and then see the times when they need more support, or calling a parent, or giving the student extra tutoring, or giving additional support if they are falling behind."

Sun gives the example of a VLA student taking an online English course. That student could "come in for writing workshop twice a week, and that gives them that face-to-face opportunity to be in a smaller classroom environment, and also to work with the teacher and be able to ask questions and be able to get some individualized help."

VLA students are offered a myriad of activities from which to choose, from student council to going to the same prom as the PFAA students. Sun says VLA students "have very different activities that give that social aspect [of a traditional school]."

Star Academy is the fifth academy at Natomas Charter School. It is an elementary school serving around six hundred TK-5 students. Star uses a teaching method of differentiated, small-group instruction that allows teachers to meet individual student needs. Teachers take an integrated curricular approach by creating standards-based thematic units of instruction. The core subjects of math, science, social studies, and English use a hands-on inquiry-based learning approach.[9]

Natomas Charter School has significantly outperformed both the Natomas Unified School District average and the state average on California's state standardized tests in English and math.

The school has won various prestigious recognitions, including a *US News and World Report* award for being in the top 10 percent of high schools in the nation. The *Sacramento Business Journal* has also ranked it the #1 high school in the Sacramento region. Such achievements are even more impressive, said Sun, when one considers that the school has a huge range of different kinds of students with very different kinds of needs . . . And some of those differences do not necessarily show up on the demographics."

"I think the students who gravitate to us," said Sun, "tend not to have been successful in the traditional system." As Sun pointed out, "when students come to our school, they find a niche, and I think they feel a sense of community and sense of belonging."

Parents who have voted with their feet to send their children to the school give the Natomas Charter high marks. Sun says, "we've had 93 to 94 percent satisfied and very satisfied with the school, which is not surprising if you choose the school, you are probably going to be satisfied with it."

What about the teachers at Natomas Charter? What kind of person wants to teach at such a different type of school? Sun answered:

> We've been very lucky in attracting great people to our school. I think that's one of the reasons why we've been successful all these years. And because our mission is so different, and each of the academies are so different, we tend to attract people who want to teach in that environment where they have a lot of flexibility and they have the opportunity to create. . . We get ones

who come out of ed school who tend to be the ones who want to try something different. They don't want to just go into a traditional system. We've also got veteran teachers who say, "You know what, there's got to be a better way." So, it really varies.

And those teachers who did not fit? Sun observed:

We've had folks who haven't worked out because they come in thinking this is a traditional school, and then they realize, "Wow, you mean I have to create my own curriculum?" Yeah, that's one of the basic tenets. We don't just hand you a textbook and you do from chapter one to twelve. So, we tried hard to make it clear what the expectations are.

Natomas Charter School uses a performance-based system to determine teacher salaries. Rather than the typical school-district uniform schedule where all teachers receive the same incremental salary increases based on years of employment or units earned, Natomas Charter has teachers develop a portfolio based on the school's expectations for teachers.

Sun says, "In the portfolio they gather evidence and present that portfolio to a panel of peers and other administrators." This panel then decides if the teacher moves up the salary schedule. "We have professional-level benchmarks that are in place, and then a demonstration before they can jump to that next level."

In the usual school-district teacher contract, says Sun, "You take a step in column, and the way you go to the next column is you take a bunch of units, and it doesn't have anything to do necessarily with what you teach." In contrast, at Natomas Charter, "We collapse all the columns, and so instead of moving across horizontally, you keep moving vertically until you hit the next level." The vertical movement to the next level, though, is based on "this demonstration portfolio rather than just taking a bunch of units of credit." Ultimately, she says, "We provide feedback and support and all that, but if a teacher is not working out, we let them go."

Natomas Charter School is one of the truly unique charter-school models in the nation. Its five academies offer parents and their children an incredible choice of instruction and learning systems within an umbrella school of choice. If any school embodies the *Choosing Diversity* theme, it is Natomas Charter.

## CLASSICAL ACADEMY

Cameron Curry is the affable, ebullient, and dynamic executive director of the Classical Academy charter schools in San Diego County, California. Walking into his office is like walking into a pop culture art gallery.

A huge painting of actor Gene Wilder as Willy Wonka hangs over his table. A Willy Wonka costume, complete with purple frock coat, hangs from the ceiling. A framed Star Trek uniform signed by Captain Kirk himself— William Shatner—adorns the wall opposite Gene Wilder. Memorabilia from TV-show toy cars to action figures of Leonard Nimoy and Barack Obama to Planet of the Apes movie posters decorate the room.

It is not your typical school administrator office, but, then again, Classical Academy is not your typical school.

Started in 1999, Classical Academy, like the PACT academy at Natomas Charter School, focuses on homeschool parents who want a partnership with a charter school. Starting with a relative handful of families, the school now has more than 4,500 TK-12 students at campuses in several San Diego County cities, plus those who access the school online.

Curry, whose career ranged from working as a city economic development director to working for the Greater San Diego Chamber of Commerce, was the first board president of Classical Academy. Married to a school teacher, the couple were instrumental in getting the school approved by the local board of education.

In an interview with Curry, he told me that at the outset there was a small group of homeschool parents who wanted to be involved in their children's lives and education, but who also were looking for accountability and for a way to work with a credentialed teacher. Charter schools and choice gave them that opportunity, said Curry:

> For different places, you get to have choice. But in public education, there isn't really choice in our community. And those families who come from a place of means have always enjoyed [choice]. But in our district, for the elementary alone, there's nineteen thousand students. There's one way of education and isn't it time we offer families choice in our community? And based on that the board took public comments, and then the board voted to approve the charter.

The school, says Curry, partners with parents through T-C-A: trust, collaboration, and accountability. "We trust that parents and their guardians," he says, "have the best interests of their students at all times," and that parents "are the primary educator and teachers are there to support them in that effort."[10] Also, "We collaborate with parents to create the best personalized academic program for their student."[11] Finally, "Parents and teachers hold each other accountable to ensure that we are working to benefit students in our care."[12]

What does this partnership between parents and the school look like in operation?

For grades kindergarten through eighth grade, Classical Academy offers two options: an independent study program with optional enrichment labs and an independent study program with two-days a week in a workshop setting for grades kindergarten through six grade and three-days a week for seventh and eighth grades.[13]

Jennifer Morrow, the principal at Classical Academy Middle School in Escondido said that the reason for increased availability of on-campus classroom time in middle school is that parents start to feel uneasy teaching their students more difficult subjects like algebra.

"We love the two-day model," says Morrow, "but we also feel like as you get ready for high school, we need to do something more, and so our parents helped us develop the three-day program."

The middle school has two different programs under its umbrella. One program, called M-Track, is, says, Morrow, a more traditional program, where "kids rotate between their five classes." The second program is the Summit program, which uses the learning program provided by the Summit charter schools (Summit charter schools will be profiled in a later chapter of this book). The Summit program emphasizes the concept of mentorship, which involves, says Morrow, "one-to-one support and coaching from a mentor." Students learn through self-directed learning (SDL), that is, the content on their own with the support of credentialed teachers and their parents. Students have projects that are their bigger assignments, "where they're mastering cognitive skills" that are "deemed important to learn for them to be successful."

Morrow says that there is some friendly competition between the two programs, but, collaborate together. The students are on campus three days and home two days and then they have breaks and lunch all together.

So, there is choice within a school of choice.

For Classical Academy High School, the school blends classroom-based study with independent study. All programs are 100 percent independent study, and within the independent study model, optional personalized learning programs include:

- Studio
  This program allows students to take all of their courses on campus Tuesday-Friday under the direction of a highly qualified, appropriately assigned, single subject credentialed teacher.

- Online
  Students are enrolled in online classes with face-to-face and virtual access to credentialed teachers, opportunities to come on campus for standards-based lessons, [advanced placement] reviews, and science labs.

- Family
  This program allows students to take all of their courses off-site under the supervision of their parent or guardian with the guidance of a highly qualified credentialed teacher.

- Monday Learning Labs
  Students from all programs are able to meet with highly qualified credentialed teachers for tutoring, grade recovery, or content review.[14]

Once again, there is choice within a school of choice.

## The Homeschool Parent Experience

Although students may be homeschooled part of the time, Curry says, "we're providing all the packets, all the materials, all the information, all the curriculum, all the tools, everything you need." He uses the example of a second grader and says that material given to parents is not published material. The school pulls together materials from an array of sources, thus creating their own standard and curriculum.

The school is flexible where learning takes place. There are workshop/classes on campuses, but as Curry notes:

> Everything we provide here at the Classical Academy is independent study, and workshops and all that kind of stuff is frosting on the cake. But you're not required to come because then you'd be a five-day classroom experience and that's not who we are. That's not who we want to be.
>
> We want to be able to . . . meet the individual needs of individual students. One student needs to be in a classroom. I need that accountability. I need to be with somebody a couple days a week to hold me accountable.
>
> We have done a lot over the years with parent training. . . But we provide so much support and encouragement and tools and resources and all kinds of stuff for parents. They really feel empowered to be the primary educator for their students, because that's our core belief as an organization. Mom and Dad, you taught your sons and daughters how to walk, you taught them how to put on their shoes, you can teach them algebra. And we're here to help.

Classical Academy also has an online high school. Dr. Stacey Perez, the online school's principal, said that she meets with every family:

They can personalize this education any way that fits them as long as they're on a graduation plan. So, I meet with a family, they will choose their classes, whether they want to be on campus two days a week. They can come on campus up to four days a week, but workshops are schooled Tuesdays and Thursdays for freshmen and sophomores and Wednesdays and Fridays for juniors and seniors. Sometimes those overlap into a four-day program if they're taking a higher level class as a sophomore.

"So, for two days a week or the structured workshops," said Dr. Perez, "that's when they're working on projects, collaboration, limited instruction, because they're getting that online through their playlist." Teachers "actually offer them a playlist of about ten different resources that they can look at, to find out the same information."

Some students may choose to work exclusively from home for "social emotional needs, because they are traveling musicians, they're in sports," but there is "some reason they don't fit into a traditional classroom five days a week and they need more options." Dr. Perez said, "we're finding they're very successful in the self-directed learning part."

For the students at the online high school, there is a large common area where they can do their self-directed learning activities. There are always credentialed teachers in there, a couple of lab supervisors, and support staff if needed. "It's just an open area with flexible seating," so "they can sit wherever they want as long as they're directing their own learning."

"So, when they get to a concept they don't understand or a problem they might need help with," explained Perez, "they can go up to a teacher, who will be roaming in the room and who will come to them."

"Yes, you get to work at your own pace," observed Curry, "because you may be gifted in [an] area and so you're going to move through the curriculum rather quickly, which is great, but you're really struggling in writing so you need more one on one." In the online common area, "there's a credentialed teacher right there at your disposal." "You're still doing the online program, however, we're standing next to you and helping you achieve."

Classical Academy also stands next to students through cohort mentoring. Each teacher has twenty-five students that may or may not be in one of their core classes. "And they're building relationships with those students," said Perez, "and they're asking the questions: 'Why are you here? What's your story? How can I help you? What are your passions?'" "Having these conversations," she believes, "is an important part of the personalized approach." Morrow, the middle school principal, said, "the cohort person really becomes the keystone to the kids' success."

At all the Classical Academy campuses, the school ensures accountability through regular parent-teacher conferences held every six weeks to go over the performance of students and to decide on ways to improve achievement. Teachers review the work of students and discuss what students have learned from their assignments. If students are not completing assignments or are showing deficiencies, students will be required to see teachers more often. As Curry noted, "if you're not completing your assignments, then basically you're truant."

If students continue to fail to complete assignments, then the principal becomes involved and "then that's really when we press mom and dad." It may turn out that the student may need a more structured five-day-a-week traditional school program because an independent-study program is too loose for him or her.

To parents, Curry asks, "Do you understand that this is a partnership we share with you? . . . We're going to collaborate to make sure that your son or daughter gets the best education possible, but at the end of the day, we're going to hold each other accountable."

Teachers place student work samples into audit files, plus fill out forms that attest that students have completed their assignments. It is these audit files, says Curry, that generate the average-daily-attendance funding for the school. Not keeping track of student work completion and learning indicators ends up getting "independent study in all kinds of trouble when you don't do that."

### Educational Philosophy

Classical Academy emphasizes strong foundational skills, which means that students must understand the rules of the basics: Phonics, grammar, spelling and mathematics all have rules. Every student is taught the rules and how to use these rules on a regular basis. A student cannot be expected to run before he walks. He or she cannot engage in reading comprehension and analysis until learning how to read well. Critical problem solving is dependent upon a knowledge, understanding, and practice of the basics.[15]

In English language arts, as soon as students are able to read, quality classical and modern literature will be used as the core reading program.

Curry says that that the school's belief that different students have different learning modalities underscores why students should take advantage of the on-campus workshops that the school provides:

> You're sitting down and having those individual discussions with students to say, "Oh, you learn best if you're touching it; oh, you learn best if you're watching something; or you learn best if you're actually collaborating in a group with other students." That's why you need to come in and be a part of these workshops. This is

why you need to be on campus two days a week because this is going to basically individualize what we're doing for you.

For those who think that schools like Classical Academy just focus relentlessly on core subjects, the reality is that students have a wide variety of electives from which to choose. Morrow says, "we don't just do the core subjects, we also really believe in the whole child, and so we're really proud of our elective programs." Students at the middle school "get five electives throughout the whole year."

The electives are six-weeks long, which gives them a wide variety of exposure to different subjects. Students may think they did not initially want to take a particular elective class, but, says Morrow, "then they end up loving it because they didn't know they could play ukulele or do 3D printing and be successful at it."

Prior to becoming principal at Classical Academy Middle School, Jennifer Morrow was a parent who "went to all their introductory information meetings, and just got hooked on the philosophy of partnering with parents and the blend of classroom instruction plus homeschool." "I just thought it was the best of both worlds," she says. Evidently, Classical Academy parents still think that philosophy is a winning one.

In the school's 2018 parent survey, 94 percent of parent respondents rated the Classical Academy school that their children attended as meeting or exceeding their expectations.

Cameron Curry recounted the time he first stood before the local school board in the late 1990s to advocate for the approval of Classical Academy's charter petition: "I really just stood before the board and said, what makes America great? You have the opportunity to go to any movie you want, a different movie theater, and you can get your hamburger from different places—you get to have choices."

That ability to choose is what America needs in education as well, and it is that choice that will meet the differing needs of parents and their children and make American education great.

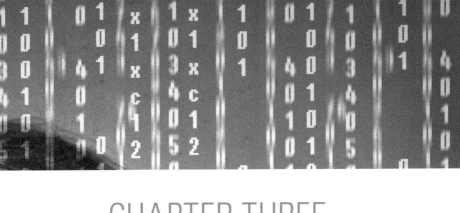

# CHAPTER THREE
## High-Tech Charters

" *This is going to be a place where people accomplish things that seem beyond their reach, where you run into a problem rather than away from it, where you continue to do the unexpected and where people live dreams that seem too big to dream.*

~ DR. KEN MONTGOMERY
EXECUTIVE DIRECTOR,
DESIGN TECH

# High-Tech Charters

## DESIGN TECH HIGH SCHOOL

MIA IS A high school junior who came back to public education. "I went to a lot of different private schools all across the [San Francisco] Bay Area," but they "just seemed more like a prison." "I didn't like how they were teaching," she recalled, and "I didn't like the kids." Then an amazing change occurred.

Mia and her younger sister Cara were both admitted into Design Tech High School, a high-tech public charter school in Redwood City on the Bay Area Peninsula. "It was the best choice I ever could have made for myself," says Mia. Cara agreed, saying that the school "would be a good fit for me."

Located in a sleek modern building on the beautiful Oracle campus, the high-tech business giant, Design Tech is the only public school based on a corporate campus in California. Enrollment at the school is capped at five hundred fifty students, who are selected by lottery, which ensures a diverse student population.

"This is a lottery school," said Cara, so, "I feel like we get so much diversity." She observed:

I see people with so many different interests and everybody can learn from each other. We all have different interests in all different harmonies. We can teach each other things that other people might not know they're interested in, and I feel that's so important to the student body. And they all came from the lottery and almost everyone is such a good student and really does contribute to the new tech community.

The school has a predominantly minority population, with 60 percent non-white students. Students are drawn from more than thirty cities in the Bay Area.

Founded in 2014, Design Tech says that its educational model "emphasizes knowledge in action and extreme personalization." Technology, observes the school, has transformed much of society, giving us more choices than ever before. Yet, use of technology in education is lagging and needs to be used to transform schools and give students the choices that they experience in other parts of their lives.

### Design Tech's Personalized Approach

The school bases its learning program on the four core principles of design thinking: empathy, radical collaboration, building to think, and testing prototypes. Upon these principles, the school believes it can unleash each person's creative potential and work in an environment that is engaging and productive for students and staff.[1]

Teachers meet students where they are and then help them not only to master content, but also apply their knowledge in an authentic way.[2] To complement this teaching philosophy, the school says that the curriculum meets students where they are and offer[s] them a personalized approach to learning so that their talents, knowledge, interests and skills are maximized.[3]

Technology, says the school, can facilitate this educational philosophy when teachers use it to personalize content to student needs and place cutting-edge tools in the hands of students.[4] Further, new learning technologies also allow students to interact with content, get instant feedback on their work, and be 'tutored' by computer programs." These technological developments give Design Tech "the opportunity to deliver content and instruction that are tailored to student needs."[5]

The school says each student is given their own personal Chromebook rather than textbooks. "The Chromebook online learning management system allows teachers to regularly review data on their performance," which "in turn allows teachers to coach students and personalize instruction."[6]

As one example of how the school uses technology to deliver instruction, Cara said that as freshmen they had to take a class on prototyping, "where we had to build a house with this online software." The assignment involved a lot of geometry, and, "I feel like that was a really good use of technology . . . using our resources to really visualize the learning instead of just having a two-dimensional piece of paper."

In addition to technology, the school delivers instruction in a variety of ways, depending on the individual needs of the student: small group instruction, blended/online learning, or one-on-one tutoring. As opposed to the teacher's traditional role as a "sage on a stage," Design Tech teachers act as facilitators and coaches, "reviewing student progress through the curriculum each day and determining whether or not the student's chosen modality is providing them with the best access to academic success."[7]

Mia appreciates the instructional methods of Design Tech's teachers. She cited her "incredible English teacher," who "doesn't become more like a lecturer, but becomes more of a mentor and guides us." Her sister Cara agrees saying, "I feel I can bounce ideas off of the teachers and the students, not just having these teachers talk to us just saying this is this."

One of the amazing innovations at Design Tech is its policy of allowing students to actually create curriculum and teach classes using that curriculum. I spoke to Thomas, an upperclassman at the school, who has both designed curriculum and taught classes. He said that a new teacher at Design Tech asked him to put together a curriculum for a class that he was going to teach at Stanford University in the summer of 2017. "So, he and I worked together on developing a curriculum," he said, "and we actually co-taught it during the Design Lab [at Design Tech]." Design Lab is a course that focuses on designing solutions to concrete real-world problems.

Thomas said that through co-teaching, "I gained a lot of experience with how to teach a class, how to build a curriculum, and the fundamentals of design thinking." He explained that much of the design thinking at Design Tech is based on the work of the Stanford University design school. The multi-step design process, which includes empathizing, defining an idea, prototyping, and testing, was created for engineers, not necessarily for high school students. He observed:

> The issue is that nowhere in that process are they really actually going through the entire process in a cohesive timeline. And while they'll understand each step of the process individually, they're useless out of context with each other. So, what we're doing is we want to pull away from that five-step method and try to come up with a design that's just more intuitive and straightforward for the students and something that just feels a lot more connected.

In addition, Thomas and a friend designed a new curriculum for one of the school's design courses that addressed their view that the previous curriculum was too structured.

He and his friend taught the course in March 2018, "and it was very well received."

I interviewed Thomas while he was teaching a design class. He said that the course he was teaching used the curriculum he had created with some updates:

> The intention of the classes is to have as little structure as possible because we want these students to discover their most intuitive approach to design thinking, because it is a little bit different for every person. That doesn't mean that we can't provide some sort of guidance and initial instruction. So, at the end of the March class, we shared the entire lesson plan with all the students in the class and asked them to leave comments, feedback, anything they thought was good, anything they thought could be improved . . . We got a lot of valuable feedback from that, and we included many of those suggestions and criticism in this new curriculum.

Design Tech is very open to implementing student-designed solutions. "We're encouraging the students," said Thomas, "that if you have a problem, and if you come up with a solution for it, the issue is not going to be implementing it because the school will be very willing to help you with it."

Technology assists this instructional process by creating an efficient use of time so that teacher and student can use the time savings to engage deeply in the content and focus not only on understanding the content but truly mastering it by applying it to multiple contexts. Further, technology is used to personalize instruction by allowing students to progress in their courses based on demonstrated content mastery rather than seat time.[8]

## Design Tech's Personalized Learning Philosophy

Since each student has different needs, each student has an individualized learning plan.

Personalization in learning at Design Tech is not limited to instruction but extends to student scheduling. Students are able to take advantage of a flexible scheduling policy. Thus, although students must be on campus for a full school day every day, a student's daily schedule will be determined by academic needs. For students needing extra help, for example, teachers can schedule small group lessons with similarly situated students.[9]

Mia, for instance, takes advantage of the flexible scheduling to play tennis. She says, "So I have this time after my four core classes to go and play tennis, and it was designed just for me." "I feel like [the scheduling] is very tailored to me," she says, "and I really love how they are really understanding with the students."

All this personalized learning is geared to making students into design thinkers. All students are required to enroll in a design advisory class where they learn about the design-thinking process and undertake design challenges that ask them to solve real-world problems.[10]

The design-advisory courses are a four-year set of courses. They are organized into four levels:

1. *Fundamentals of Design Thinking*: This course allows students the time to understand and practice the discrete elements of design thinking, which include: empathize, define, ideate, prototype, and test...

2. *The Design Thinking Process*: Once the elements of design thinking are understood, students will return to the full process, putting all the pieces together to approach design challenges...

3. *Engineering and Creating*: After that, students focus on using the design-thinking skills to engineer and create artifacts or solutions. At this point, students will start to identify problems in their communities and work with teachers to craft their own design challenges...

4. *Entrepreneurship*: Finally, students engage in entrepreneurship, including social entrepreneurship. Entrepreneurship requires students to not only define a challenge and design a solution, but to then communicate their vision to others....[11]

Mia says that for her, design thinking is about "creating something you're passionate about, and it's also thinking about how the user will like it—really designing something for the user, and not just for yourself." Cara believes that the design-thinking process is "really centered around empathy." "Instead of being prompted with a problem," she says, "we have to figure out a problem that our users have, so we have to figure out what's the issue in our community."

Also, Cara says, students must do more than just say a problem can be fixed, they must figure out "how we can fix it." Doing interviews with potential users and doing research is a big part of the process, "and I feel I learned what [users] want and combine it into something I'm passionate about creating."

One of the signature programs at Design Tech is Intersession. Held four times a year for a period of two weeks each, Intersession gives students the opportunity to participate in a Design Lab program, taught by core-content teachers, and Exploration Courses, which include electives, required courses for graduation such as Visual and Performing Arts, mandatory courses in health and wellness. One interesting feature of Intersession is that non-faculty individuals, such as industry professionals, may teach the courses.

During one Intersession, Mia took a course on fashion and clothing design. She went on a field trip to San Francisco where students met with a business executive who discussed the difficulties of running retail stores. "We also did interviews with people about clothing," she recalled, "which really also [gave us an] idea of how difficult it is to make clothing."

Cara noted that it is during Intersession that Design Tech students get the opportunity to interface with Oracle employees. "Especially during Intersession," she said, "we would go over to the Oracle campus and interview the workers about their jobs, what would make their jobs better, and then we will design something for that." Further, Mia noted, "Oracle employees just completely volunteer themselves to teach coding classes for students and also building robots, which is amazing for people who want to go into that field." "Oracle," she observed, "is really just completely loving and fully supports us."

To fulfill the Performing and Visual Arts requirement, Mia is taking classes in dance, but there are also options such as film, photography, and animation.

Design Tech uses a competency-based learning system, which is different from the time-based system used in most traditional schools.

Design Tech says that competency-based learning allows for deeper understanding of material and ensures that students have a basic understanding of key concepts. Importantly, the school says, "It is impossible to coast through an assignment." The school quotes one student who said: "At my last school I could just throw something together at the last minute, turn it in, get a grade and move on. Now if I just throw something together, the teacher gives it back to me and says do it again."[12]

Thomas told me, "I was really excited when I came here." At his previous traditional public middle school, he felt restricted by the school's one-size-fits all methods: "I understood the material very, very easily, and I would always do well on my tests, but the raw amount of unnecessary busy work and unnecessary repetitive actions to practice problems was so frustrating." "Coming here," he said, "was such a refreshing change because . . . you have to reach competency."

For the core classes in both the humanities and STEM, Design Tech presents courses to students in learning cycles in which there are opportunities to develop their comprehension and skill before attempting a performance task to demonstrate mastery . . . Students can progress through the concepts independently or seek additional support if challenged."[13]

On California's standardized tests, Design Tech scores well above the state average. In English, 71 percent of the school's students score at or above proficient versus the state average of 49 percent. In math, 62 percent score at or above the proficient mark versus the state average of 38 percent.[14] But again, as important as test scores are, there are other perhaps more important arguments for charters like Design Tech.

Design Tech is a leader in changing the way we look at how our young people learn and can receive their education. While so much of the traditional public school system is impervious to change, Design Tech embraces change. What Design Tech will look like in five, ten or twenty years will not only be different from what the school looks like today, it will be light-years different from what the regular public schools will continue to look like. "So, everything here at this school," noted Thomas, "is, in a certain sense, constantly evolving because nothing ever really stays the same."

"Personally," he said, "I believe that if students aren't able to change their brand new, constantly evolving charter school, if they can't make an impact here, how can they personally think that they can make an impact in the world on a larger scale?"

Thomas said that at Design Tech he had gained valuable and vital communications skills, critical thinking skills, and problem-solving skills. "I'm confident that I will be able to bring those skills and make myself more appealing to employers or to schools when I go out and apply."

Dr. Ken Montgomery, executive director of Design Tech, says, "This is going to be a place where people accomplish things that seem beyond their reach, where you run into a problem rather than away from it, where you continue to do the unexpected and where people live dreams that seem too big to dream."

So why is Design Tech successful? Is it the personalized learning? Is it the Design Thinking process? Is it the competency-based learning model? The success of the school is probably due to these and the other factors described in this section, but I believe that the key is that all of these factors have combined to create a palpable enthusiasm for learning among Design Tech's students.

When I observed classrooms at the school, students were intensely engaged. They were intently discussing the subject matter with each other, brimming with ideas, and interacting deeply with their teachers. Compare this bubbling enthusiasm at Design Tech with the lethargy and lack of interest of students in many regular public schools and one immediately understands why Design Tech is working for the students who choose it.

Writing in *Research in Higher Education Journal*, Kaylene Williams of California State University Stanislaus and Caroline Williams of the University of Wisconsin, Madison point out, "Student motivation is an essential element that is necessary for quality education." It is very apparent when students are motivated to learn: "They pay attention, they begin working on tasks immediately, they ask questions and volunteer answers, and they appear to be happy and eager." Basically, "very little if any learning can occur unless students are motivated on a consistent basis."[15]

Williams and Williams observe that there are five key ingredients that impact student motivation: the student, the teacher, content, method/process, and environment.

At Design Tech, I saw all of these ingredients in action. Because students chose the school, as opposed to being forced to attend, they were interested and valued the learning they received at Design Tech. The teachers were intimately responsive to students and were, as the students with whom I talked indicated, inspirational. The content taught at Design Tech stimulated students, who told me that what they learned was pertinent to their current and future needs. The process of learning at Design Tech was truly inventive, encouraging, interesting, and relevant to students. Finally, the environment at the school was very personalized and empowering—indeed, what could be more empowering than having students like Thomas teach classes?

"Motivation is when dreams put on work clothes," say Williams and Williams.[16] In my visits to Design Tech I saw many dreams at work, which is why the school works.

No wonder then, that Mia told me, "this school is way more perfect for me."

## SUMMIT SHASTA PUBLIC SCHOOL

"I would say that [Summit Shasta] definitely made me into a better person and it's something that's made me really passionate about education and how people are taught," observed Helen So, a bright, articulate and deep-thinking recent Summit Shasta graduate who I interviewed.

Helen was originally set to attend her local regular public high school, but heard about Summit Shasta from a neighbor, checked it out, and thought it was "innovative because they were talking about things like self-directed learning and mentorship from teachers." "I thought that that would be really good," she noted, "because it wasn't really something that I had access to in my public school."

Founded in 2003, Summit Public Schools is a network of charter schools in California and Washington State. Summit Shasta, which is located in Daly City on the San

Francisco Bay Area Peninsula, is an unassuming set of typical school buildings, but within its walls the unique Summit learning process takes place.

"We are living in a post-industrial age," according to a Summit white paper, "but our public education system still reflects the careful design of an earlier era." In contrast, Summit says it represents an alternative to this industrial model of education.[17]

The Summit program is based on students demonstrating mastery over four domains: content knowledge, cognitive skills, habits of success, and sense of purpose.[18] The foundational component of Summit's learning process is standards-aligned core-subject content knowledge, which includes "a set of vocabulary, ideas, events, concepts, properties, and details related to a given academic discipline."[19]

Summit Shasta says, "Content knowledge is the set of facts and information that is fundamental to understanding the world around us."[20] How do teachers teach content knowledge at Summit? The keys are so-called focus areas:

> The focus areas are developed across the grade spans on a developmental continuum. Students are introduced to similar Content Knowledge topics in different grades, with increasing levels of complexity and depth.
>
> Completion of all power focus areas in one course is required for advancement to the next course.[21]

The focus areas in high school are the core standards-aligned subjects. To facilitate learning in the focus areas, students have access to the Summit Learning Platform, which is an online platform containing playlists of various resources. Summit Shasta explains:

> At Summit Shasta, students have access to a wide variety of resources to help them learn relevant

content. Summit teachers curate these resources and organize them into online playlists that introduce each topic and link to videos, slideshows, websites, readings, and practice worksheets. Students engage with these resources and choose the best ones to help them learn both at school and at home.[22]

In order to use online technology, students at Summit Shasta are issued a Chromebook, and which they use at school and at home.[23]

Students progress at their own pace during blocks of time called Personalized Learning Time (PLT). As students learn the content they are assessed online as well:

> Content is assessed through online, on-demand, multiple-choice content assessments. When a student believes s/he has mastered a topic, s/he can request to take a content assessment as long as s/he is in an appropriate testing environment. The assessment is graded instantly by the computer. Students decide which content they study, whether to try again if they haven't passed it, and whether to attempt different content assessments.[24]

Helen said that at the end of studying each playlist, she took a ten-question quiz which required seven to eight correct answers to pass.

Summit Shasta says that PLT is especially important for attaining content knowledge because "students are able to accelerate or take more time and focus on learning the content that is most appropriate for them in a way that best fits their learning style."[25]

The Learning Platform is an online dashboard that allows students to set goals, track their progress, and direct their own learning by accessing the resources that make up the Summit curriculum.[26]   The Platform was developed in partnership with Facebook and is used every day by Summit students, teachers, and families.

In her freshman year, Helen completed all her playlists by December, "So I was able to work ahead in all my classes and pay attention to the projects that we were doing." "So, I think that's one of the huge advantages of the online platform," she observed, "that we get to go ahead."

However, Helen did add that there are students "who don't necessarily respond to intrinsic motivation, so they might go off track, in which case, hopefully, the teacher will see that they may be talking to classmates or browsing the Internet and remind them that they should be doing the playlists." She says, "I personally appreciate this time to get ahead in my classes," but she acknowledged, "sometimes it was easy to look around at the people who weren't being productive and be influenced by that."

As students progress at their own pace, teachers serve as facilitators, guiding students and identifying those who need additional support and intervening. Students who are advanced can access more challenging areas that allow them to delve more deeply into content.[27]

Content knowledge is critical to developing critical thinking and cognitive skills: "Each subject area has a set of facts that, if committed to long-term memory, supports problem-solving by freeing working memory resources and illuminating contexts in which existing knowledge and skills can be applied."[28]

Once students have a grasp on content knowledge, they can progress to acquiring cognitive skills, which are higher-order thinking skills that students need to solve complex problems. Summit students develop cognitive skills in every subject and in every grade level.

Summit has established a Cognitive Skills Rubric, which contains seven domains: textual analysis, using sources, inquiry, analysis and synthesis, composing/writing, speaking and listening, and products and presentations.

Within these seven domains are thirty-six different cognitive skills that range from asking questions to interpreting data and information. Summit says that these various skills enable students to be successful in college and career readiness.[29]

Commenting on this rubric, Helen said, "I think that was important to helping us improve because there would be specific rubrics on specific cognitive skills such as organization, for instance, or oral presentation." Further, "the rubrics will tell you not just how to achieve a certain grade, but even how to get past that grade."

When she submitted a piece of work for feedback, Helen would write down what score she thought she should get, while the teacher would respond based on the rubric. So, "there's a space to discuss cognitive skills using certain feedback from the rubric that you wouldn't really have otherwise."

Summit Shasta says, "Cognitive skills are taught, practiced, and assessed through project-based learning." Courses at the school "are built around authentic, real-world projects where students solve complex problems, often in collaboration with their classmates."[30]

One of Helen's favorite projects was a presentation that involved both her history and English classes. So, she said, "both of those teachers would provide guidance on this project and we would be graded by one of those teachers." Looking back, she said, "I think the concept of combining several courses into one was really interesting because it allows the teachers to work together and provide different types of feedback."

Helen did warn that she had friends who would "take advantage of that personalized learning time or save their work for the last minute because we often have more than a month to do some projects."

All projects include a series of checkpoints, or opportunities for feedback from teachers, peers and the student.[31]

Cognitive skills are assessed multiple times per year across different subjects. Students' cognitive skills development is measured on a zero to eight scale, with a six signifying college readiness.[32] At Summit Shasta, cognitive skills are worth 70 percent of a student's grade in a core academic class, while content knowledge is worth 30 percent.[33] In math, instead of using cognitive skills, understanding math concepts is worth 70 percent of the grade.

The third pillar of Summit's learning program are the 16 Habits of Success, which are the social and emotional skills that enable students to be successful at both academic and non-academic pursuits.[34] These habits range from self-direction to resilience to growth mindset to social awareness/relationship skills.

These Habits of Success are promoted in several ways. First, there is a weekly mentoring meeting between a student and his or her mentor teacher. In both mentoring and in projects, students must be self-directed. Self-direction at Summit involves a student setting a goal, planning how to achieve that goal, learning what is needed to know, showing evidence of what has been learned, and reflecting on the process.

Helen thought the concept of mentors was "amazing because there was the promise that your mentor would be with you throughout the four years of your high school career, and that person would be able to get to know you personally and guide you and be there if you need someone to talk to."

"Personally," she said, "I think I had a pretty good experience." "It was not that easy to open up to my mentor," she confessed, since she came from a regular public school. However, "having that designated time to check-in with a mentor and having them actually come up to you and ask, 'Hey, can we check in for 10 minutes?,' was really helpful to me."

She does say, though, that some of her classmates had mentor teachers who left the school before the end of the four-year period. Thus, these students might get multiple mentors over that period of time. Helen, however puts this situation in perspective, pointing out, "while I do think that having four mentors in four years isn't what was promised to us, it's still better than not having a mentor at all or being in the public school system where you have two counselors for a one-thousand-six-hundred-person school."

The fourth and final pillar of the Summit learning program is a sense of purpose. Students develop purpose through goal setting, interacting with a mentor community, and expeditionary learning.[35]

The Summit Learning Platform is critical to goal setting. Through the Platform, plus conversations with teachers and mentors, students connect their long-term aspirations, such as college acceptance, with the actions that they must take in the short-term. For example, because students need to be proficient in cognitive skills to be accepted to a top university, the Platform "enables students to track how their current levels of proficiency connect to their future aspirations." Thus, "students are able to understand how what they are learning today will directly prepare them for their goals they aspire to for tomorrow."[36]

Specifically, the Platform hosts "agendas that mentors and mentees can share." The agendas facilitate rigorous and consistent check-ins between the two. Further, the Platform "allows students and their teachers to review both academic progress from the week and the goals and learning strategies that students used to achieve them." For families, the Platform allows them to "see what is being discussed during the mentor check-in and the underlying student results that motivated that conversation."[37]

The mentor community is made up of the teacher/mentor, the student, and the student's family. At the beginning of every school year, a meeting, led by the student, is held with this mentor community to review previous long-term goals and to establish or revise year-long and long-term goals.[38]

Summit students take elective courses called Expeditions. These Expedition courses, which are two-week courses held four times a year, cover a wide range of topics from video and film production to engineering to graphic design to the college application process and many others. Also, "Summit students develop customized off-campus internships as an Expedition, where they conduct internships with local businesses, non-profits, hospitals, and other community organizations."[39]

For her Expedition classes, Helen took choir for two years, and "later on I had an amazing psychology course." "I think that in general," she said, "the expedition courses can be a good experience because they're supposed to replicate the typical job experience."

To evaluate students' sense of purpose, Summit uses portfolios of student work, reviewed by an advisory board of key adults in a student's life, and an oral presentation/defense.[40]

### Strategies for Struggling Students

When Summit students are struggling, the school employs two different strategies:

> Summit Reads (SR) and Summit Solves (SS) are dedicated times for students to strengthen their reading and numeracy skills...
>
> During Summit Reads, students read articles or practice specific literacy skills. Depending on their reading level, students may use a program like Newsela or Reading Plus. While students are reading, teachers check in with students, read alongside them, and

ask questions. The online programs provide teachers with data that they use to monitor student progress, target specific instruction, and differentiate reading materials to meet student need.

During Summit Solves, students work with targeted math curricula based on their skill level. Teachers provide each student the right level of support. While students are working on the targeted curriculum teachers coach them on relevant learning strategies. Instruction is often supplemented with small group learning or other instructional strategies designed to give students quick, targeted feedback. Depending on their level, students may use a program designed for targeted math remediation or acceleration such as Khan Academy or ST Math.[41]

Struggling students at Summit Shasta have at least ninety minutes of Summit Reads and ninety minutes of Summit Solves per week. For students who need extra help only in math or only in reading, these interventions may be scheduled more flexibly to meet individual student needs. Students needing Summit Reads and Summit Solves are grouped with students who are at similar reading or math levels. These interventions are led by project teachers and learning specialists.[42]

Summit Shasta actively partners with parents using mentors as the primary liaison about information regarding their children and the school. Mentors reach out to parents at least once per quarter and more frequently if a student is struggling.[43]

Parents may also use the Summit Learning Platform for "real-time access to what their child is working on at school and how they are performing."[44]  With this information, parents can hold their own children accountable.

At Summit Shasta, test scores are well above the state average. In English, 87 percent of students score at or above the proficient level versus the California average of 49 percent. In math, 51 percent of the school's students score at or above proficient versus the state average of 38 percent.[45]

Helen was very honest comparing Summit Shasta with traditional schools: "I do think that in terms of material, I could have learned more at a traditional school, but in terms of critical thinking and seeking help and having all these resources, that's something that I may not have had."

When I asked Helen what her parents thought of Summit Shasta, she said, "I think they liked it a lot." For a variety of reasons, "I think they really appreciate it." Other parents have similar reactions.

Christine Talivaa Aguerre heard about the school from a friend and ended up sending her daughter to the school. "It was the best thing that happened to our daughter."[46] Christine said that Summit Shasta is "Nothing like my old high school."[47]  And that's the point—charter schools give parents the opportunity to choose a learning experience for their children that is different and which meets the individual needs of their children.

Survey data show that more than nine out of ten Summit parents believe that their children are acquiring the knowledge and skills needed to succeed in college and career.[48]

Summit Shasta validates the view of parents. In 2017, the school celebrated its first graduating class with a full 100 percent of inaugural graduates being accepted into four-year colleges and universities.[49]  Not only do Summit graduates attend colleges and universities at very high rates, they also persist and graduate with degrees. Summit alumni are twice as likely to complete college than their peers.[50]

Summit's use of personalized learning and education technology in its educational model is critical to its success. Traditional public schools are also using computers and other technological tools but are not having the success that Summit charters are having. The reason for this discrepancy is likely because charter schools allow these tools to be used in a truly revolutionary way.

In his excellent 2016 report on Summit, David Osborne of the Progressive Policy Institute noted, "In the world of blended learning, Summit is known to be on the cutting edge." He then makes a key observation: "Traditional schools also use educational software, but they rarely have the freedom to reinvent their entire educational process."[51]

Others make the same point. Michael Horn of the Christensen Institute, who is one of the nation's top experts on education technology and innovation, says that when it comes to using education technology the difference between charter schools and regular public schools is that while charter schools have used technology "to transform their entire schooling model," regular public schools "use it 'at the fringe,' without changing their schedules or dominant learning methods."[52]

Further, says Horn, "the charter schools using blended learning . . . have produced impressive student outcomes that are concrete and objective." In contrast, such clear and measurable outcomes "have been missing from many of the district schools adopting blended learning."[53]

Indeed, when one looks at Summit charters such as the Summit Shasta, one sees a school that uses education technology, personalized learning, and project-oriented methods to revolutionize the school day, the way teachers teach and interact with students, the way students access the curriculum, and the way students are assessed. In too many regular public schools, education technology is an add-on or is simply shoehorned into a pre-existing 19th-Century instructional model.

Thus, the Summit learning model may be revolutionary and may prove over time to work for many students, but it is only through the freedom that a charter school gives that such a model could be implemented. That may be the key lesson for policymakers to remember going forward.

# CHAPTER FOUR
## Classical Charters

" *O give me a home where the buffalo roam Where the dear and the antelope play. Where seldom is heard a discouraging word And the skies are not cloudy all day.*

~ HOME ON THE RANGE
(AMERICAN FOLK SONG)

# Classical Charters

## JOHN ADAMS ACADEMY

EVERY MORNING AT John Adams Academy charter school, students gather around the flagpoles outside the school's buildings, say the Pledge of Allegiance, and then sing a patriotic song. "Home on the Range," which I had not heard sung since I was a child, was the song chosen for the day I visited the school's campus in Roseville, just outside Sacramento, California. The students sang the song with enthusiasm, led by one of their own.

Located in several glistening buildings in a business park next to the local interstate, John Adams Academy in Roseville is a K-12 charter school that opened in 2011. John Adams also has campuses in two other Sacramento-area suburbs. Founded by businessman Dr. Dean Forman, who had also served as president of the local school board, and his wife Linda, the school's mission and vision statement says: "John Adams Academy is restoring America's heritage by developing servant leaders and defenders of the principles of freedom for which our Founding Fathers pledged their lives, fortunes, and sacred honor."[1]

"America's heritage," says the school, "is a tradition of a free society of self-governing citizens." A free society "is necessary for true human flourishing—life, liberty, and the pursuit of happiness" and is grounded "in the principles of liberty and freedom embodied in the Declaration of Independence, the Constitution of the United States, and the Bill of Rights."

Dr. Forman told me in an interview at the school's Roseville campus that parents "love the emphasis on the founding era, and that it's okay to believe that America is a great place and to be patriots."

To implement the school's vision, John Adams Academy has developed a three-pronged model consisting of classical education, core values, and servant leadership training. According to the school, "American classical leadership education is distinct from modern educational systems in both structure and content." Classical education is based on a so-called "trivium," which is Latin for the "three ways" that, in this case, are comprised of grammar, logic and rhetoric:

> [T]he classical model of education is to teach first the "grammar" or basic ideas, skills, concepts, language, and methods of a given subject before encouraging pupils to explore the "logic" or inter-relatedness of such concepts . . .
>
> The final stage of classical education is that of "rhetoric" or the art of persuasively expressing to others the implications of the knowledge they have acquired through the first two stages of learning.[2]

In addition to this classical form of instruction, the content at John Adams is also classically based. Students, who the school refers to as "scholars," will "read and study the greatest works, or 'classics,' of the Western Tradition." In addition, "Scholars will investigate great American works highlighting the principles of liberty, virtue, morality, entrepreneurship, and democracy."[3]

John Adams Academy emphasizes the study of history, philosophy, and government, especially the individual's role in preserving freedom. Teachers "help scholars make connections between subjects to show how they converge into a single whole called 'truth.'" Teachers guide students through modeling and Socratic dialogue.[4]

A classical education is also language intensive, demanding students use and understand words, not video images. It is history intensive, giving a comprehensive view of human endeavor. Finally, it demands self-discipline.[5]

Some may ask, why read classic works? John Adams responds saying that classic great books, which are imbued with great themes, noble language, and universality, "open our eyes to the true nature of our world and take us across the divide that separates mind from mind," "teach us about human nature," "bring us face-to-face with greatness," and "force us to quietly study, ponder, analyze, think, ask, discover, cry, laugh, struggle, and above all feel, change, and become."[6]

"A classic," says the school, "gives us the personal wisdom to be better as an individual and citizen of a free nation."[7] The classically educated student, therefore, "not only learns wisdom but becomes wise from living the principles resulting from intensive study, immersion in the classics and the application of this education to improving the world."[8]

John Adams Academy uses the classics, where possible, rather than textbooks. Textbooks are secondary sources that are "thoughts about thoughts." In contrast, classics "begin where thought itself must begin: in the original context." Further, textbook authors act as filters, whereas the school wants students "to encounter the classical works firsthand, deriving their own opinions about the original texts."[9]

At the K-8 level, John Adams Academy uses a combination of *Junior Great Books*, the *Story of the World*, and the

Core Knowledge Sequence, along with CPM Math, Saxon Math, and Systematic Phonics. The curriculum at this level is adapted to the needs of young learners, and "introduces scholars to the key concepts to be explored in great depth as they prepare for critical thought processes necessary to successfully navigate the rigor of the curriculum of the middle and high school years."[10]

At the high school level, John Adams uses the classics as the foundation for student learning. For example, in the 10th grade, the school provides a sample list of texts, both classics and textbooks that reflect the types of works that are used in its high school curriculum, with texts ranging from *Dante's Inferno* to da Vinci's *Art and Science,* More's *Utopia* and Rousseau's *Social Contract.*

The school argues that by studying the classics students develop a greater degree of maturity, judgment, and understanding of human nature and the ability to think independently than perhaps any other educational activity. [11]

A classical education at John Adams means not only learning about ancient classical civilizations, understanding the ideals of America's founding era, and reading great classic books, but also includes being exposed to classical languages: "Exposure to Greek and Latin provides great depth in the ability to speak well and write convincingly."[12] Not only does knowing Latin make it easier to learn English vocabulary, because Latin is the foundation for much of English, it also makes learning another language such as Spanish much easier.[13]

Some people may wrongly believe that a classical education is just listening to the teacher, reading old books, memorizing, and repeating back lines. Nothing could be further from the truth. As students learn classical content, teachers use the Socratic method of questioning and discussion, rather than mere lecturing, to create a deeper understanding of great works and content knowledge.

Joseph Benson, executive director at John Adams Academy, told me that he sends several of his children to the school. He said that that the Socratic method "really makes them engage the text" and "lights the fire so they become their own learners." He sees this result in his own children, observing that his daughter "has become empowered in her learning" and his sons "are doing one or two books a week on their own just because they love reading so much and are engaged so much that it just becomes part of who they are."

When I sat in on a history class at John Adams that was covering the Greek gods, I witnessed a very revealing discussion between the teacher, Josh Beidel, and one of his students on the role of the god Apollo. When he described Apollo's place among the gods, a student responded by disagreeing and giving a nuanced description of Apollo's role and oversight. The Socratic method encourages this type of dialogue and deeper thinking on subject matter.

After describing this incident to Benson, he said that at his own dinner table his fourth grader and his ninth grader, who both attend John Adams, recently had a Socratic discussion on the Greek myths, and he and his wife just watched in amazement and satisfaction.

The Socratic method is used even with very young students. Second-grade teacher Lindsey Singleton told me, "Most people think it's impossible to do a Socratic seminar with second graders and it is not." "I do Socratic seminars," she said, and "they learn to speak with each other." "Everyone is respectful agreeing and disagreeing," Singleton noted.

Heather Brown, headmaster of the elementary education at John Adams, said that the school hires "a lot of teachers who come to us straight out of teacher preparation programs." They come to the school thinking in a box created by their credentialing program. But under the learning program at John Adams, she says that teachers have an epiphany, "where they can say, wow, I not only improve their skill set, but this child is on fire and I can't stop this passion." Further, "teachers have come to us and said, 'the kids just keep asking for more.'"

"You see this kind of spark and this inspiration," she said. And, referring to the discussion of Apollo that I witnessed in class, "that's the fire and I think that's probably what you saw today in that Socratic discussion." Brown said that you think that you want to reach a certain point with the students, but "most of the time they take us three times farther than we ever anticipated because they get excited and they get passionate about it."

For example, Rosemary Groth, who teaches secondary-level history, says that her students will read Mark Twain's "Joan of Arc" very intently because the class re-enacts Joan's heresy trial. Students are given roles in the trial, so they really get into the reading. "They want their evidence," she said, "because they want to win."

The culmination of a student's education at John Adams is the Senior Capstone project, which consists of the Senior Service Project, the Senior Thesis and Defense, and the Senior Speech. Seniors take a Senior Capstone course to provide them with the time, instruction and support necessary to complete the three components.[14]

The Senior Service Project "displays the scholar's commitment to Servant Leadership." Students identify a need in their community and address the need through a targeted project.[15]

The Senior Thesis is a fifteen to twenty page academic thesis "which critically engages one or more of the classics a scholar has encountered at John Adams Academy." Students are expected to come up with "a meaningful question of fundamental importance to mankind for research, conduct the necessary investigations to adequately answer the question, and then present the findings of their investigations in a logically sound, rhetorically persuasive paper." The student then defends the paper in front of a panel of teachers.[16]

The Senior Speech is a ten to fifteen minute speech where students share what they have learned at their time at John Adams. Students deliver the speeches to an audience of other students, faculty and staff, and community members invited by the students. Students are encouraged to view the speech as "an act of statesmanship, by which they are to inspire those in attendance to become better members of their families, communities, organizations, and country."[17]

The second prong of John Adams' learning program is the school's 10 Core Values, which include appreciating America's natural heritage, fostering creativity and entrepreneurship, and high standards of academic excellence. Because it sees itself as preparing future leaders through a principle-based education, the school seeks to integrate these core values into the curriculum.

These 10 Core Values are infused throughout the curriculum at John Adams, even for the youngest students. Kate Linares, who teaches kindergarten, said, "I teach about Columbus because I think it's the perfect way to teach all the 10 Core Values to kindergarteners because here we have a person that was showing entrepreneurial spirit and just really stuck to it." However, after he reaches his goal, "we see a shift away from public and private virtue."

"You set a goal," she observed, "and so many people attain that goal and then because they have success they shift and that virtue that they started with is gone."

"I think it is good for [scholars] to start to see that there is truth," said humanities teacher Melody Van Tassell, "not that we know it absolutely in every case, but there is something to strive for and that you can actually know things."

The third prong of John Adams Academy's learning program is servant leadership training. Servant leadership involves four interrelated components: 1) the focus of leadership is on promoting the good of family, community, and country, above self, 2) service to others is incorporated into the curriculum, 3) scholars study the lives of servant leaders throughout history, and interact with community servant leaders through our mentoring program, and 4) scholars model and practice leadership through simulations, historical reenactments, mock trials, etc.[18]

"A servant leader," says the school, "is a servant first, driven by an inner compass of virtues or core values, with a natural desire to serve and empower others." Importantly, "This is not about being subservient but about sincerely wanting to help others by identifying and meeting needs."[19]

As an example of servant leadership in action, Dr. Forman tells the story of a young man who had attended John Adams Academy for a number of years, and who moved to Connecticut with his family. The young man heard about a young veteran who had come back from serving in the military with mental and emotional trauma. He engaged with the young veteran and decided to make a difference, so he started a school club to honor the men and women who had served their country and who were suffering from trauma. He wanted to get these veterans engaged in school so they could find purpose again.

"As he did that, I thought, this is exactly the kind of person we want," observed Dr. Forman.

At John Adams, developing these servant leaders does not occur by teaching a certain set of facts, by training in a particular skill, or through some dictate from the administration. Rather, the school says that servant-leadership development is a process rooted in the principles of freedoms, whereby individuals are inspired to take responsibility for their education; to grow from nurtured to self-governing, responsible, and virtuous; and to progress from self-improvement to selfless service. Key to this process is mentoring.

## Working with Struggling Students

The coursework at John Adams is not easy. Students are constantly challenged. Despite hopes and expectations, some students will struggle like they do at other schools. Nevertheless, the school points out that it is designed to serve all students, including those who would be at risk of achieving Standard Not Met proficiency on state exams.[20]

For struggling students, the school has developed a comprehensive "Response to Intervention" program that identifies these at-risk students based on state tests, classroom assessments, and performance on class assignments. Once identified, the school provides targeted intervention by teachers and staff who identify, assess, track, and remediate at-risk students in order to ensure the progress of any who are failing to thrive in the academic environment.[21]

Progress of at-risk students is monitored weekly to monthly to guide instruction within the "Response to Intervention" program and to assess the skills targeted for intervention. Also, formative assessments are done daily and used for decision making within the intervention process.[22]

The school uses a testing program called i-Ready that gives teachers growth data on student performance and individualized instruction. "I like i-Ready," says second-grade teacher Lindsey Singleton, "because it's showing me progress." The program gives teachers information on where students are weak "so that I can better support them and I can grow my kids."

In addition, for those students not meeting grade-level standards on classroom assessments, remedial intervention before school, after school, and on Saturdays are offered. Teachers assigned to remediate students are those who have proven instructionally strong in this designated area.[23]

In examining John Adams Academy's learning program, some may still wonder if the education that students receive at the school actually prepares them for the 21st-century marketplace. It is easy to see how high-tech-oriented charter schools, mentioned in the previous chapter of this book, prepare students for our modern world, but are students who receive a classical education at a charter like John Adams just as prepared?

The school anticipates this skepticism and counters: "When a scholar leaves John Adams Academy knowing how to critically read, effectively write and communicate, do math, connect with history and know *how* to think, that scholar can easily be trained in any specific job skills they may need in the field of their choosing. They will have learned *how* to learn."[24]

Scores of John Adams students on the SAT bear out the school's confidence in their learning model. In 2015-16, the average composite SAT score for students at John Adams Academy in Roseville was 1676, considerably higher than the 1550 that the College Board pegs as the college-readiness benchmark. John Adams' average score placed it among the top three high schools in Placer County, where the school is located. Also, the school's 1676 average score was more than 200 points higher than the 1455 California statewide average on the SAT.

Indeed, the education at John Adams is not just about having read Shakespeare or knowing the amendments to the U.S. Constitution. In the end, the education at the Academy develops life skills that are critical to the future success of its students.

"By helping scholars master these and other life and leadership skills," says the school, "they become leaders, analysts, entrepreneurs, and statesmen."[25]

Norman Gonzales, the director of outreach at John Adams, points to President Thomas Jefferson: "He had a mentor; he received a classical liberal arts education; he became a scholar; he controlled his own learning; and he went off and learned every subject he thought he might have an interest and passion."

"We're not trying to do a conveyer-belt education—make kids do specific things," he said, "We're really looking to give them the tools and skills necessary to be successful in whatever endeavor they choose."

John Adams Academy is a perfect example of a charter school whose test scores are not earth-shattering, but where parents vote with their feet for the school. Math test scores are somewhat above the state average and English scores are at the state average.

One's first observation is that any state standardized test is not testing much of what students at John Adams are learning. There is therefore a strong possibility of a disconnect between test performance and the true level of learning of a John Adams Academy student. Further, whatever the school's test-score performance, parents have demonstrated, from the time the school was first contemplated until today, that they want what John Adams offers.

At the first informational meeting to discuss the opening of John Adams in Roseville, the parking lot at the meeting place was backed up with cars loaded with parents and their children who wanted information about enrolling in the school. "We were blown away," said Gonzales, "because it was standing room only." "We had probably one thousand people who showed up, and the police showed up because the traffic was backing out into the street." Despite the reputation of the surrounding regular public schools as "good schools," Gonzales said there is a need for a charter school that "had a different vision of what school should be."

Today, parental demand is as strong as ever, with a long waiting list of children trying to gain admission into John Adams. The school's Roseville campus has now grown to around one thousand three hundred students. Two new campuses have recently opened in the cities of Lincoln and El Dorado Hills, both of which are suburbs of Sacramento.

Survey data show strong levels of satisfaction among parents with the education that their children are receiving at John Adams. More than nine out of ten parents responding to the school's survey either agreed or strongly agreed that John Adams Academy's "classical leadership curriculum provides a sound liberal arts education for my child(ren)'s gifts, talents, and special needs."[26] Ninety-five percent say that the school has high expectations for all students; eight out of ten say that their children's math skills have improved at John Adams; 85 percent say that their children's reading and writing skills have improved; and, despite the school's rigor, 86 percent say their children have fun learning and are excited to go to school.[27]

Ninety-five percent agree or strongly agree that John Adams "is a supportive and inviting place for scholars to learn," and 97 percent say that the school "is a safe place for my child." No wonder then that more than nine out of 10 parents would likely or very likely refer others to the school.[28]

Heather Brown gives a face to these high satisfaction rates. She described meeting with a mother of a student who told Brown that she came from a disadvantaged background where they never read any classic works. Now, Brown said, she is reading classics with her children, they are discussing the books together, "and that has fueled the mom." The mother has read *Wurthering Heights* and other classics with her children, so, "Now they're pushing; they're stretching themselves; and it's going from school to home."

Forman says, "For those who are coming here, I would say that it's based on the culture." "They come here," he believes, "because they love the culture, and when you define the culture, I would say it's one of respect of virtue."

He is no Pollyanna, however. Nothing is perfect, including his beloved country. He does not look at history, for example, with blinders. "It's not as if America hasn't made mistakes," he acknowledged, "or even started with some very glaring errors in the case of slavery." "But the beauty of [America's] system is self-correction," he emphasized. The school wants students to recognize ways that the country comes up short, but then asks them, "how would you make it better?"

"We use this word 'restore' America's heritage, and it has to be done every generation," he observed. "Every generation that comes to us."

Math teacher Martin O'Hara summed up things nicely saying, "You have a form of education that's been tested, that's been around, that takes advantage of classics and classical methods, and it's becoming mainstream." By perfecting this model and doing it well within a charter system, "you're doing a great service to parents and to Americans, and this is exciting."

## MASON CLASSICAL ACADEMY

Kelly Lichter, the founder of Mason Classical Academy, a K-12 charter school in Naples, Florida, is one of those parent pioneers who have powered the charter movement. When I asked her how she started Mason, she said, "So back in 2011, my husband and I were talking about where our one- and two-year-olds would eventually be going to school and we started looking at the local schools and I wasn't really blown away by anything and so I just started digging."

"So, I was telling my husband," she recalled, "how my dad said Hillsdale College [in Michigan] has one of the best education models." She went to Hillsdale's website, was impressed, and eventually visited the college. While there she met with Phillip Kilgore, director of Hillsdale's Barney Charter School Initiative.

According to Hillsdale College, the Barney Charter School Initiative promotes the founding of "classical charter schools and excellence in their teaching and operations" so that public school students "may be educated in the liberal arts and sciences and receive instruction in the principles of moral character and civic virtue." Hillsdale argues:

> Reform of American public education, to be successful and good, must be built on a foundation of classical liberal arts learning—the kind of learning best suited to a free society and most needed for its preservation. The Barney Charter School Initiative is an important step in that direction. . . .

When a founding group's interests and abilities are a good match with the Barney Charter School Initiative, BCSI will assist in creating and implementing the school's academic program, providing the curriculum design and teacher training.[29]

Hillsdale's Barney Charter School Initiative has now started more than twenty classical charter schools across the country in nine states. Phillip Kilgore says that the Barney Charter School Initiative "is an excellent way to reintroduce sound learning, the classical liberal-arts-based education that was common, even ubiquitous, in this country."[30]

Lichter said that after talking with Kilgore, "I came home from the trip and told my husband, I'm completely blown away by what kindergarten students would learn, what first graders would be learning—it's nothing like any other school we have. . . .So I said, we've got to bring this model to Naples." She and her husband started working with Hillsdale from that moment. Eventually, the Collier County school board approved their charter petition and Mason Classical Academy opened in 2014.

## The Meaning of "Classical" at
## Hillsdale College and Charter Schools

"A classical education," says Mason Classical Academy, "cultivates wisdom and virtue by nourishing the soul on truth, beauty, and goodness." Mason students "pursue wisdom and virtue at every grade level and in each of the many disciplines offered to our students." The school's academic focus is on "developing thoughtful, literate, and expressive high school graduates."[31]

Terrence Moore, who helped establish Hillsdale's Barney Charter School Initiative and who serves as the founding principal at a Hillsdale-associated Ascent Classical Academies in Colorado, says students at Hillsdale-associated charter schools will study "the traditional liberal arts—language and literature, history and government, mathematics and the sciences, music and art—in a coherent and orderly program." The curriculum in each of these subject areas "will run from the rudiments of basic literacy and math skills to the higher orders of thought and expression."[32]

"A classical education requires more than functional literacy," according to Moore. Hillsdale associated charter schools will teach students from early on "high standards of grammar, precision in word choice, and an eloquence that can emanate only from a love of the language." Throughout their classical education, students "will be exposed to the highest examples of eloquence attained by the greatest writers and speakers of the language."[33]

Classical education, though, is more than knowing content and being able to use that content in a skillful way. It is also about how one acts and why.

The school's so-called "Pillars of Virtues," which include: responsibility, respect, perseverance, integrity, honesty, courage, citizenship, and cooperation.[34]

"We don't have a separate character education or virtue curriculum," says Kelly Lichter, rather, these values and virtues are "really embedded within the curriculum, the books they're reading, and the characters they come across in the discussions they have in class." So, when students study historical figures they see "the challenges they had to deal with and what virtues did they have or what virtues did they not have?"

One parent writes that Mason students "memorize these eight pillars (usually a focus on one every month so that by the end of the year all eight are known), and students know their definitions by heart." If a student gets in trouble, "they are asked what Pillar of Virtue they broke and will most likely get an assignment to write out that Pillar's definition to reinforce that virtue."[35]

Hillsdale-associated charter schools provide an education, says Moore, that reaffirm America's founding principles.

The schools "will teach students that true freedom and happiness are to be obtained through limited, balanced, federal, and accountable government protecting the right and liberties of a vibrant, enterprising people."[36]

## Mason Classical's Learning Program

At the K-8 level, Mason uses the Core Knowledge Sequence curriculum, which promotes cultural literacy and provides a grade-by-grade sequence of specific topics (history, geography, literature, visual arts, music, language arts, science and math).

Kelly Lichter says that in "the elementary grades, our students are getting history, not social studies." "They're reading literature and poetry and fables," she observes, and, "They're starting to recite from memory." She is an advocate for memorization "because memorization really trains and exercises the brain so our students as young as kindergarten will get up in front of their peers and recite these poems." She says, "it's good for public speaking because they become accustomed to it."

At the high school level, the courses include a required course in British literature, three required courses in Western Civilization, and courses in Latin.

The British literature class, which is required in the tenth grade, uses a wide variety of primary works to teach students. One of the most important courses at Mason is Western Civilization 1. The school points out that knowledge from this course is essential for understanding the content in a wide array of other courses.

In its required Latin 1 course, Mason indicates that students are expected to read historical Latin works in the original language during students' time at the school and that memorization, the bête noire of modern progressive education, is crucial to learning Latin.

Some may argue that requiring students to read a large number of seemingly archaic works or requiring them to learn a "dead" language is too onerous and destroys the supposed fun of education. Mason retorts, "Assuming that a child will not be able to succeed in a challenging environment is tempting, but simply untrue." Rather, "The excitement of students beams as they become able to converse with one another in a language that most adults do not understand," while Western Civilization comes alive "for those who hunger to know about their world."[37]

While such a response may seem like puffery, the nearly unanimous glowing reviews of the school by parents bear out this picture of excited and enthusiastic students. One parent whose children had attended regular public school, virtual school, and private school, said she concluded that not only is Mason better than all these previous schools, but, "I overhear my children discussing poetry and history on a regular basis."[38] Another parent echoed these sentiments:

> We have been in public school and private school and this is the best, hands down. It seems to be a better education than the private schools and you don't have to pay for it. Our kids are so much more respectful and well behaved since sending them to this school. I thought it was going to be way too difficult because of rumors that the school was so hard. It has been the opposite. Our kids love the challenge and are happy to work harder because of it. It is amazing to go places with our kids and have them point out classical art and what era it's from. A friend asked my middle school son what his favorite music was and he replied, "classical"![39]

Another parent said that she saw the positive change in her child after only a short time at Mason:

I am happy to report that our first grader, who had zero interest in learning a year ago is now (after only a month at Mason Classical) reading, can recite classic poems and the preamble to the U.S. Constitution, he knows the seven continents, is striving in math, can point out rivers in countries across the globe, is mastering the Riggs phonics system and is showing confidence that we have not seen before, and above all he is excited to learn and he *loves* his school.[40]

Similarly, another parent observed about her son: "Within two months of enrolling him at MCA, he was excelling and enjoying Shakespeare, joined a sports club and cut back on his online gaming . . . He loves this school, the amazing educators and his newfound interest in education!"[41]

### Instructional Methodologies

Mason is focused on what happens in the classroom. The school day is structured around teacher-led direct instruction where we make the most of every educational minute.[42] Popular progressive teaching methods are scorned, while traditional methods are promoted. MCA believes in knowledge-centered education where the teacher is the leader of classroom instruction." "You will not find," the school emphasizes, "cooperative learning centers or student pods in our classrooms or observe project-based, child-directed instruction taking place."[43]

Further, "Desks face the front of the room, and our students show their respect for teachers by standing when they answer questions or address their teachers."[44] Mason has a list of what teaching is like in its classrooms:

- Teacher delivering content-specific or skill information for majority of classroom time specifically in the grammar school

- Teaching a rigorous, rich, challenging curriculum regardless of test standards
- Specific teaching precedes any expectations of students (organization, standards, etc.)
- Focus on mastery and skill building (drill, rote learning and memorization in grammar school)
- Phonics-based reading instruction – beginning in kindergarten

Mason also has a list of the types of teaching methods that will never be found in its classrooms:

- Project-based or exploratory learning
- Assignments of busy work that takes student time, but does not further learning (such as word searches)
- Teaching to the state test
- Enrichment and "fun" activities (MCA believes that learning is fun!)
- Much time wasted and lots of "down-time"[45]

One parent observes that Mason students learn via three techniques: "1) They *hear* the content as the teacher teaches it; 2) They *see* the content in writing as the teacher writes notes on the board; 3) They *write* the content into their notebooks." The parent says that students study from their own notes, which "reinforces the importance of taking full notes, in clear handwriting." Also, "it's easier for the student to study their own handwriting—they will recall when they were writing those notes while studying."[46]

"At the end of the year," the parent notes, "the students have these beautiful, worn-out notebooks full of the knowledge they learned—they want to *keep* these notebooks because they worked so hard to write everything down."[47]

The parent says, "The students are proud of their work and their knowledge—I just love it."[48]

There is empirical support for Mason's teaching methods and for parents' love for them. In her book *The Academic Achievement Challenge: What Really Works in the Classroom?*, the late Harvard University education professor Jeanne Chall reviewed a wide number of studies and found that "the traditional teacher-centered approach generally produced higher academic achievement than the progressive, student-centered approach."[49]

Chall observed that the evidence supporting teacher-centered methods was especially strong in reading and, to a somewhat lesser extent, in mathematics. In reading, teacher-centered approaches are usually characterized by direct instruction from the teacher, systematic instruction in phonics, and teacher-assigned literature and non-fiction works.[50]

While Mason uses a traditional teacher-centered pedagogy, this traditionalism does not mean that there is limited interaction between teachers and students in class. Like John Adams Academy, Mason uses the Socratic method to "open students' minds for deeper understanding of subjects."[51] Traditional pedagogy does not mean that students cannot advance according to their talents and abilities. Take math, for example. Kelly Lichter says, "students who are excelling in math can actually move ahead an entire grade level." Her daughter, who attends Mason, is a fourth-grade student, but "she is in the fifth-grade math class."

A parent echoes Lichter saying that her children are "Going ahead in math based on their ability (both have been placed one grade level higher in math based on testing they do at the beginning of the school year—this actually puts them two years ahead of the public school track)."[52]

The capstone for seniors at Mason is a twenty-page senior paper. The topic must be on an issue of fundamental importance in the Western tradition. Each senior must present his or her paper in front of faculty and the entire senior class.

Kelly Lichter says that in order to write the paper, students "go through a whole process their senior year." The seniors "really have to defend their positions as to why they believe something." "You just don't see that anymore in schools," she says.

## The Results Speak for Themselves

The results of the classical education model at Mason Classical Academy are impressive. The school's test scores in English and math are much higher than the state average on Florida's standardized test, even though Lichter says "we don't teach to the test at all."

She points out, "after four years [of existence], we are ranked number one in the district and that's over fifty schools." Mason achieves its top ranking despite the fact that district schools "are test prepping these kids beginning in the second grade" and "that's all they do year-round." In contrast, she emphasizes, "we just don't operate that way, we continue teaching our wonderful curriculum and these students are just doing amazing." So amazing that the school is among the top fifty schools in Florida, "and that's out of over three thousand schools," she says.

More than the test scores, though, is the near unanimous parental satisfaction with the school. Lichter said that on parent surveys, "it was over 92 percent overall high satisfaction rating." She noted, "most parents are extremely thrilled and happy." With such high parent satisfaction rates, it is no surprise that the school, which has more than nine hundred students, has a long waiting list.

Speaking of Mason Classical Academy and all the Hillsdale College-associated charter schools, Phillip Kilgore says, "Thousands of children attending excellent schools, having your character shaped, has exciting prospects for this country."[53]

Dr. Larry Arnn, president of Hillsdale College, says that the Barney Charter School Initiative is growing, "so this can get huge." "It can go everywhere," he says.[54] And the reason why Hillsdale's Barney charter schools and classical education can go everywhere is that parents want those schools and they want that learning model for their children.

# Photos of Schools Featured in this Book

## *Magnolia Science Academy Charter School*

## *Design Tech Charter School*

Dr. Ken Montgomery
Design Tech
executive director

## *Summit Shasta Charter School*

Lance Izumi visiting the campus of
Summit Shasta Charter School

# Classical Academy Charter Schools

Cameron Curry
executive director

Lance Izumi with Cameron Curry
executive director

# Lifelong Learning Academy

 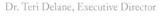 

Dr. Teri Delane, Executive Director

# *Natomas Charter Schools*

Ting Sun
executive director

# Grimmway Charter School

Principal Joanna Kendrick

# CHAPTER FIVE
## Meeting Needs in Rural America

" *Much of our [education reform] movement . . . is focused on urban areas. [But as the statistics show,] the educational deficiencies of rural America can be just as stark as those in urban America.*

~ NINA REES
NATIONAL ALLIANCE
FOR PUBLIC CHARTER
SCHOOLS

# Meeting Needs in Rural America

## GRIMMWAY ACADEMY SHAFTER

WHEN MANY PEOPLE think about charter schools, they often think of schools in the inner city of large metropolises. This image is not surprising given the fact that many of America's major cities are home to significant numbers of charter schools. Los Angeles, New Orleans, Detroit and New York City, to name but a few, have large charter-school sectors. Yet, not all charters are located in teeming metropolitan areas.

A couple of hours north of Los Angeles is the tiny town of Shafter in Kern County, which is one of California's major agricultural centers. While Bakersfield, the Kern County seat, is a medium-sized city, most of the county is flat farmland. Shafter is located halfway between two major highways, Interstate 5 and Highway 99, which pass through Kern County. The town pops out of nowhere on a country road that runs between the two thoroughfares.

When I drove to the Grimmway Academy charter school in Shafter, I immediately missed the cross street for the school upon entering the town and, within less than five minutes, was back in the orchards that surround Shafter. It is that small, and a world away from the iconic beaches, movie studios, and urban sprawl just a few hours to the south.

Grimmway Shafter is an elementary school and is the second and newest Grimmway charter school, which opened in the fall of 2017. Grimmway's first campus was established in Arvin, a nearby town in Kern County and about as small and equally rural as Shafter. The Shafter campus consists of modular buildings and a metal-frame café building. The school was built in just nine months.

The Grimmway schools are the brainchild of Barbara Grimm-Marshall, whose Grimmway Enterprises is a world-leading grower, packer and shipper of fresh, processed and frozen carrots.

In an interview for this book, Paul Escala, the brilliant and articulate executive director of the Grimmway Academies, said that the genesis for the charter schools occurred when Grimm-Marshall established a college scholarship program for the children of workers at her company and "the applications that were received really didn't speak to the level of high academic outcomes."

Grimm-Marshall then looked at the reasons for this reality and found, "The local schools that these children were attending were among the lowest performing in the state of California." Combine that fact with chronic poverty, the isolation of rural communities like Arvin and Shafter, the lack of civic infrastructure "and that really crated a dynamic that didn't provide an atmosphere for success."

She spent a few years visiting charter schools and talking to other philanthropists. Also, as the leader of a huge agricultural company, she was also concerned about the well-being of students in rural communities, who often suffer from high obesity and diabetes rates. She visited Alice Waters, famous for creating the Edible Schoolyard in Berkeley, "and really saw a marriage between a rigorous academic school environment coupled with health and wellness."

Her belief that hard work, educational attainment and the right opportunities are key to success in life, compelled her to establish the Grimm Family Education Foundation. The Foundation developed a charter petition and presented it to the local school board to establish the first Grimmway Academy in Arvin, which has a student population that is virtually all low income and Hispanic.

Escala recounted that there was considerable opposition to the proposed charter school from the local school board and the local labor organizations, "including the Dolores Huerta Foundation, the United Farm Workers, and Service Employees International Union."

The school board voted down the charter petition, but on appeal to the Kern County board of education, the latter approved the creation of the school. Thus, says Escala, "even before the school opened up, before it was even born, it was under attack, and I think that speaks volumes for the entire education reform movement and trying to create something new and something visionary that doesn't conform to the status quo."

Grimmway Academy Arvin's sister school in Shafter is an extension of the belief that poor minority children, who often come from non-English-fluent immigrant backgrounds, can succeed in life if offered the type of learning program that fits their individual needs.

Grimmway Shafter has a student body that is about 90 percent Hispanic and 10 percent white. In contrast, Kern County is 65 percent Hispanic and 23 percent white. More than eight out of ten students are classified as low income and are part of the government free-and-reduced lunch program.

Unlike urban charter schools, where children may travel considerable distances to attend a school, Escala says, "we're very intentional about being a neighborhood school; we want to be close to kids; we want them to walk to school."

The school emphasizes the importance of improving educational quality in a rural setting:

> Our vision is for Grimmway Academy Shafter to transform the educational landscape for students in the rural areas of Kern County by providing a model of excellence and innovation leading to college readiness and lifelong success.
>
> Our mission is for Grimmway Academy Shafter . . . to close the achievement gap for students in the rural areas of Kern County by creating an environment for student excellence and well-being.[1]

The school started school-year 2017-18 as a kindergarten through fourth grade school, but will add a grade per year until 2021-22, when it will become a full K-8 school. By 2021-22, it is envisioned that the school will have a student population of approximately seven hundred forty.

Grimmway Shafter opened with an enrollment of four hundred students with a wait list. There is also a wait list at Grimmway Arvin. Escala comments:

> That is a huge note to make because in many respects, the first couple years of a charter school in a relatively new community that has never been exposed to choice, the parents are somewhat reluctant taking a chance. [The charter school] is a relative newcomer, and you have multi-generational legacies at other local schools. You have sibling relationships that exist where parents are not really willing to remove their child to take them to a new school.
>
> But they did that with us. And I think that speaks volumes to our work and to our reputation.

In these small rural communities, emphasized Escala, "people vote with their feet, and the demand is real . . . we've enjoyed healthy enrollments from day one, so I think it speaks for itself—parents want choice."

## The Students at Grimmway Shafter

Stacey, Noe, Cailyn and Edgar were all fourth graders when I interviewed them for this book. All had previously attended a traditional public school prior to enrolling in Grimmway Shafter, except for Cailyn, who had attended Grimmway Shafter's sister school in Arvin.

Safety was a major concern for Stacey, Noe and Edgar specifically in their previous schools.

Stacey said that she felt more vulnerable at nearby Golden Oak Elementary School. Her parents specifically chose Grimmway Shafter because of their concerns for Stacey's safety. She now feels safer attending Grimmway Shafter.

Noe had previously attended Sequoia Elementary School. He said that at his old school there was no supervision of students at recess. It was during such times that he was the victim of bullying. And it was because of this persistent bullying that his parents wanted a new school for him and chose Grimmway Shafter. Now, because Grimmway enforces an anti-bullying policy and offers many anti-bullying resources for parents, and because he says that Grimmway Shafter ensures adult supervision at recess, he is much happier at his new school.

It is interesting and important to observe that while analysts and researchers may focus on statistics and academic policies, students like Noe are much happier because of something as seemingly small as adult supervision at recess, but which has big consequences in terms of feelings of personal safety and consequent ability to focus in the classroom. In other words, if children are worried about their safety, how can one expect them to concentrate fully on their coursework? Conversely, if children do feel safe, then they can focus on their studies and enjoy the process of learning.

Edgar offers a more extreme example of the safety issue. He told me that he felt less safe when he attended Golden Oak Elementary School. He related that the gates were not secure at Golden Oak and outsiders could easily come onto the campus. Edgar then described an incident when a man came on campus, tried to get into the school office, and was eventually shot by police officers off campus. Edgar said the man had a weapon.

Listening to Edgar's voice and seeing his facial expression as he told his story underscored what a lasting impression that incident had on him. He is now acutely aware of safety measures like locked gates. He said that he liked Grimmway Academy because he feels that the school is more secure.

It cannot be stressed enough that these children feel safer at their new charter school. Regardless of issues of academic performance, parents should be able to choose a school solely because it is safer for their children. And researchers need to always bear in mind such crucial non-academic issues when judging charter schools.

In addition to safety, the students also indicated that health issues figured into their parents' decisions to send them to Grimmway Shafter. One of Grimmway Shafter's signature programs is its garden program. The school sits on eight acres of land and students grow a wide variety of fruits and vegetables on campus, including squash, corn, tomatoes, carrots, snap peas, kale, watermelons, strawberries and more. These foods are then used to feed the students, and all students take a kitchen class.

Molly Sowers is the school's kitchen teacher. She teaches the children about why certain foods are healthy for them. She then supervises them as they prepare meals, which include salads, green garden tacos, peach salsa, and popcorn from school-grown corn. She says that her students often share recipes with their families. The garden program and the healthy eating habits it promotes is what drew many parents to Grimmway Shafter.

Noe told me that the food at his previous traditional public school, Sequoia Elementary School, was not healthy. He said that his parents wanted a healthy diet for him and, therefore, Grimmway's garden program was a significant factor in their decision to enroll him in the school. Stacey also liked the garden program. She said that she enjoyed the food from the garden and likes trying new things to eat.

Barbara Grimm-Marshall and the Grimm Family Education Foundation support various community health and wellness initiatives, including those at Grimmway Academy Shafter. Paul Escala calls the garden program, "the core of what we do, it's who we are." "We put the garden in the middle of the [Shafter] campus," he says, which symbolizes that the garden program is "really at the heart of what we do." The program, he says, has many facets:

> We're seeing that kids are appreciating the health and wellness environment we're creating. And that's really done in three ways. It's done in our garden, in our instructional kitchen and in our café. Every student participates in the garden and in the kitchen on a regular basis. Every kid is eating from our café. Our café has a salad bar, so we can teach kids how to build a salad from everything we make from scratch.

Students are not allowed to bring unhealthy foods like chips and candy to school. That rule also applies to the adults who work at the school. All faculty and staff have café privileges as part of their benefit package, which, Escala says, "encourages our teachers and our staff to eat with our kids at lunch." Escala also points out that the school teaches "soft skills," such as "how to set a table, how to take down a table, and how to converse over a meal." These soft skills teach "collaboration, teamwork, and the value of community."

The school also promotes healthy eating to parents and to community members through health-and-wellness fairs, where produce from local vendors is sold at a discount. Family cooking nights are held, where families come and learn how to make healthy recipes. Like safety, health concerns do not show up in standardized test scores. Yet, they are part of the reason many parents in Shafter decided to choose Grimmway Academy for their children.

Overall, twice-a-year surveys show that parents at Grimmway Academy Shafter are extremely satisfied with the school.

### Grimmway Shafter's Academic Program

Grimmway Shafter's principal, Johanna Kendrick, says, "Our focus is to support our students in their growth, both academically and individually." The school does that through "small class size, and our unique blended learning model [which] allows for learning across a range of environments and experiences—in the classroom, in the Learning Lab, in the garden, and through enrichment programs."

"We are continually reinterpreting the learning experience," she says, "so that every child at Grimmway Academy is engaged, happy, and successful." Kendrick points out that given the success at Grimmway's Arvin campus, where student scores on state tests topped those of surrounding traditional public schools, "we have demonstrated that high achievement is possible among students from rural areas who have often been overlooked by education reform efforts."

Kendrick discussed the key factors at Grimmway Shafter, such as blended learning, the Learning Lab, the school garden and other enrichment programs that have made the school a success. First, Grimmway realizes that quality teachers are crucial to quality education.

"But we're looking for passion," observes Escala, "and we want people who want to challenge the status quo."

Teachers are evaluated through ongoing observation throughout the year and regular consultations with administrators and peers. Escala says, "if our teachers are underperforming, it's not just their responsibility, it's the responsibility of our leadership teams on campus to make sure that teachers are performing well."

Some teachers are not invited back, he says, "so it's a rigorous, intentional process." High performing teachers can see receive one-time bonuses.

Beyond having all teachers with the requisite credentials, the school uses a so-called "teaming approach" with its instructional staff. As opposed to the ordinary one-teacher classroom model most traditional public schools use, under this teaming approach, teachers have their own instructional homerooms, but students move to different teachers throughout the day:

> The students in grades kindergarten to third grade have one teacher each day who focuses primarily on literacy instruction, one teacher who focuses primarily on social studies and science instruction, and one teacher who focuses primarily on math instruction. The students in grades four to six have one teacher each day who focuses primarily on literacy instruction integrated with social studies and one teacher who focuses primarily on math instruction integrated with science.[2]

"This teaming approach," says the school, "allows the teachers to develop deep subject matter knowledge and an ability to diagnose and intervene with even the most struggling students."[3]

A good friend of mine is a teacher in a traditional public school in the Sacramento, California area. She recently complained to me about the lack of parental involvement and engagement at her school, with parents feeling little responsibility for their children's performance or behavior. Like many charter schools, Grimmway Shafter says that deep community involvement is a school requirement.

The school's teachers do home visits with every family during first grading periods of the year and expects significant parent attendance at school meetings. The school emphasizes, "In order to achieve our extremely high expectations, it is crucial that our families help us to motivate their students to do their homework, come to school alert and prepared, and reinforce Grimmway Academy's values."[4]

Grimmway Shafter requires that each student create an individualized learning plan (ILP) with his or her homeroom teacher and parents. These plans set specific goals and actions for children so that they can meet academic benchmarks.

In discussing individualized learning at Grimmway, Escala explains that the school looks at various student assessment results and then customizes instruction on an individual level, "so if Johnny has demonstrated and excelled in a certain subject matter or in other areas has not, we can customize their instructional plan to address those specific areas of growth."

For literacy instruction, students are grouped based not on their grade levels or age, but on their content knowledge. So, Escala says, "we may have a cohort of students in a particular reading block that might be a mix of third, fourth, and fifth [graders]." "It depends on their level of knowledge and performance," he says.

The school uses a "Response to Intervention" model, which provides four tiers of intervention for students in need of additional assistance. "Regular cycles of interim assessment results are analyzed to identify students who are failing to make adequate progress in reaching the charter school's goal for significant gains," and then, "[Individual learning plans or ILPs] are updated to reflect areas of strength and weakness and explicit classroom modifications, areas to target in our computer curriculum, and specific goals and methods for tutors."

The first tier of intervention occurs in the classroom and school's Learning Lab:

> Guided reading groups are used to deliver these more individualized objectives during normal classroom instruction. [The school] conducts Learning Lab throughout the day, in which each class of students rotates through literacy and math computer centers. In the computer center, a student's interim assessment results are used to create a specific online intervention program for that student by the Administration and teacher.[5]

All Grimmway Shafter students attend the Learning Lab for 80 minutes per day. Google Chrome and Google Classroom are used. There are weekly assessments in regular classrooms and based on the data from these assessments, students get the help they need in the Learning Lab. The Lab has one teacher, a teaching assistant, and two special education teachers.

Edgar and Stacey, two of the fourth graders I interviewed, told me that Learning Lab was their favorite class. Stacey said she got to practice on things with which she was having difficulty. Being able to improve her skills and knowledge increased her self-esteem and confidence. She also liked the educational games that improved her learning. "When things are hard, you learn more," said Stacey, whose comment evidenced wisdom beyond her age.

The second tier of intervention is the instructional success team, "which occurs in small groups within the Learning Lab, where students are grouped based on their specific needs." Learning Lab staff initially deliver intervention curriculum and collect data on student progress, which they share with the classroom teacher.

Grimmway's thinking regarding how best to use the Learning Lab has evolved. At the Shafter campus today, Escala says:

> We saw the opportunity to take a cohort of students, say ninety students, and break them into groups . . . [S]tudents would be grouped by subject matter, whether it was reading or math, but instead of sitting at a stationary desk and looking at a desktop computer with headphones on, kids are in front of mobile technology and are able to rotate through that space in a more flexible environment. So, [instead of] sitting in front of a screen for ninety minutes, you may be sitting in front of a screen for thirty minutes and then have a one-on-one breakout if, for example, you're an English-language-learner kid and you need to have more time in conversational discussions.

The third tier of intervention occurs when students in tier two fail to make adequate progress in achieving significant gains in their performance. These students enter the student success team process and continue to receive tier-two support plus additional accommodations in the general education classroom.

If these tiers of intervention do not produce the expected result, then the school has yet another intervention strategy:

> If Learning Lab, small group instruction, and classroom accommodations fail to help a student make adequate progress, the Student Success Team meet to determine possible referral to special education assessments. This allows the

student to receive individualized attention and the services of specialists.[6]

The school believes that providing these various levels of intervention allows them "to serve the most struggling students more effectively than traditional elementary schools."[7]

Grimmway Shafter's typical student is a socioeconomically disadvantaged English learner who is one-and-a-half years behind his or her peers. Thus, the school uses an extended day schedule from 7:55 AM to 3:40 PM, plus an optional two hours after school. The school says, "we give our students extra school time to catch up academically."[8] The goal is to get all students achieving at or above grade level by the time they leave the school.

After enrolling at Grimmway Shafter, students are tested using a number of different measurement tools to determine the level of student performance relative to grade-level standards. If students are detected through the assessments as having problems or difficulties with understanding, a number of steps are taken.

First, their individual learning plans are revised to direct their work during intervention time. During intervention time, students work directly with an instructional assistant on the specific skills they are lacking. Thus:

- Instructional assistants are provided with a very specific eight-week plan combining suggestions from the classroom teacher and Administration in terms of strategies and approaches to use to get a student to meet their target at the end of eight weeks.

- In six weeks, when the school assesses again, measurement is done to see if meaningful progress has been made by the student receiving the intervention services.

- Students not responding to interventions will be referred to the school's student success team, which will identify specific goals and target skills that will be addressed through targeted intervention each day. Again, the students will be assessed every six weeks to determine growth and the need to modify goals.[9]

## *Core Subject Instruction*

Grimmway Shafter prioritizes reading above other subject areas in the early grades and for students who are still struggling in later grades. In practice, this prioritization can mean that a student is pulled out of a content area class for individualized reading instruction or an [individualized learning plan] for a student which allocates them a double block of reading if necessary.[10]

As important as the amount of time devoted to reading, however, is how the school actually teaches reading. The school says they are firm believers in the findings of the National Reading Panel.[11] The Panel, which was a congressionally mandated independent group of fourteen experts, issued its findings in 2000.

After reviewing all available high-quality research that could be generalized to the entire population of American students, the Panel found five types of reading instruction that improved students' reading skills: phonemic awareness (the knowledge that spoken words are made up of tiny segments of sound, referred to as phonemes), phonics instruction, reading fluency, vocabulary, and text comprehension. Of these, the Panel said that the most important was phonics instruction.

Although some school districts have come to view the Panel's findings as old or no longer relevant, key experts disagree. University of Illinois at Chicago professor Timothy Shanahan, one of the nation's top reading and literacy experts, says, "most of the studies of phonological awareness, phonics, vocabulary, oral reading fluency, and reading comprehension strategies completed since [the National Reading Panel] have tended to confirm the generalizability of the findings to an expanded range of students (e.g., younger kids, older kids, second language learners)."[12]

Since the school has a large number of students who are not fluent in English, a significant amount of small group time in K-2 is spent on oral language acquisition and fluency for our [English learner] students, and on phonemic awareness and phonics skills leading to grade-level reading fluency.[13] In grades 3-8, students who are performing at grade level will have mastered most aspects of oral language, phonics, and phonemic awareness, and are focused more on deep vocabulary investigation and comprehension of fiction and non-fiction texts.[14]

Grimmway Shafter uses the Fontas and Pinnell Benchmark Assessment System, which is a running record assessment that measures a student's basic fluency and comprehension in grade-level texts. This assessment program gives the school baseline data on a student's reading proficiency.[15] In addition, the school uses the Dynamic Indicators of Basic Early Literacy Skills, which is an assessment that provides in-depth information on a student's area of needs in English language arts. This assessment allows the school to further tailor a student's individual learning plan to the student's individual learning needs.[16]

Writing is the natural complement to reading. At Grimmway Shafter, students begin writing from their first day at school, but writing can be a real challenge for students not fluent in English because Grimmway Shafter requires a demonstration of understanding of language rather than the more simple recognition of words and sentence patterns (which are required for success in reading).[17]

The school uses the Northwest Regional Laboratories 6 Trait Writing Model, which includes six factors characteristic of excellent writing:

- Ideas: The content or main theme can be looked at as the heart of the message.
- Organization: The internal structure of the writing.
- Voice: The personal voice of the author comes through which can give a sense of a real person speaking.
- Word Choice: The use of precise, colorful and rich words to communicate.
- Sentence Fluency: The writing flows together often with a rhythm or cadence.
- Conventions: Mechanical correctness, including spelling and grammar.[18]

The school adapts these six factors in order to give students specific feedback on their writing.

Writing at the school is taught as part of the literacy block. In kindergarten, writing is connected to the read-aloud, while by the second grade a structured workshop for students is conducted focusing on brainstorming, organizing, drafting, editing, revising and creating a final draft.[19]

In math, students focus not only on finding the correct answers, but are expected to articulate *how* the answers were derived. Noe and Cailyn, two of the fourth graders at Grimmway Shafter, told me that STEM (science, technology, engineering and math) were their favorite subjects at school. Cailyn, for example, said that she loved learning new things in math such as decimals and fractions.

Echoing what her classmate Stacey said about the school's Learning Lab, Cailyn said, "When it's too easy you don't learn as much." Noe said that the way STEM is taught at school allows him to stay positive.

In math, the school's method includes hands-on activities, classroom discussion about mathematical reasoning, and sufficient practice in calculation to make arithmetic operations automatic.[20] The importance of making math operations "automatic" cannot be understated. In an important review of experimental research, University of Illinois researchers analyzed the data on how humans process information. They found:

> When prior learning is automatic, space is freed in our working memory, which can be used for comprehension, application, and problem solving.[21]

Grimmway Shafter uses the Bridges math curriculum and College Preparatory Math curriculum. The math program at Grimmway Shafter emphasizes number sense, which includes "linking symbols to quantities, understanding part-to-whole relationships, and being able to make calculations with the same fluency that we stress in reading, so that [students] can devote more of their thinking to visualizing and tackling difficult word problems."[22]

Ultimately, says the school, the central goal in math is to prepare students for algebra. Critically important to achieving this goal is hiring the right teachers: "We believe that because we hire teachers who want to teach with a focus in math, we are able to find teachers who are generally more fluent and more passionate about the teaching of math than most elementary teachers."[23]

Since Grimmway Academy schools have large numbers of students not fluent in English (English learners), the school has strong thoughts on how to teach this significant subset of students. For nearly two decades up until 2016, California did not allow bilingual education for English learners. Then, a ballot proposition in 2016 was passed that allowed local school districts to choose bilingual education, where children are taught in their native language and supposedly gradually transition to English. Previous evidence in California showed that few students transitioned into English fluency under bilingual-education policies.

Structurally, the school runs a full inclusion program for EL students. These students are not sheltered in bilingual instructional classes. Rather, from the first day of school, EL students are immersed in English with the Spanish language support they need to learn the language and develop the grammatical framework and vocabulary needed to begin developing as readers and writers."[24]

English learners are monitored by homeroom teachers using the same individualized learning plan process as other students:

> Because Grimmway Academy focuses on each student individually, we will be able to accommodate a much wider range of levels of literacy. For example, our reading classes will be broken into multiple groups. ELs will be the majority in all groups in kindergarten and first grade and constitute at least one group in subsequent years. This will allow teachers to then focus on instruction in language acquisition at the current level of each student. In addition, because online curriculum in the Learning Lab can be tailored for each student, ELs will have even more time to practice their English in a one on one setting. While we would not normally not endorse rote learning exercises, these exercises are effective in areas like initial vocabulary acquisition for ELs . . . ."[25]

The school uses Rosetta Stone and Renaissance Learning's English in a Flash curricula.

To measure English learner progress, the school uses the

ADEPT assessment program, which measures a student's growth in language proficiency. The exam is administered in January and at the end of the school year. The ADEPT assessment allows teachers to give input on the language development of their students and also provides them with information regarding specific language skills that they need to address and practice.[26]

The school then uses standards from the state exam for English learner development and ADEPT to help teachers to calibrate their instruction appropriately for a student at different stages of language acquisition. The school employs the following strategies:

> In language arts, we believe that oral language comprehension and production is the critical link allowing [English learner] students to make large gains in reading and writing. Thus, much of our Literacy blocks in the early grades will be focused on oral language development and comprehension activities. This will be made possible through the individualized or small group instructions that occurs during guided reading. Through this small group, a student will be able to receive specific language instruction, allowing them to further develop their language proficiency through re-tells, explicit vocabulary lessons, and a small group focus on letters, word patterns, spelling, blends, sounds, etc. In addition, during this guided reading time, the staff will provide an [English learner] center, which will be focused on specific language activities (picture cards, writing, vocabulary, development, etc.) that are targeted to specific categories of students based on their progress on ADEPT.[27]

Further, for struggling English-learner students, there are interventions that "focus specifically on English letter/sound correspondences, word patterns, spelling rules, and other skills." The school believes that by "introducing these skills in isolation and practicing them in context, students are better able to move through the language proficiency categories."[28]

Grimmway's English-learner strategies are working. Escala says, "because we have been so successful in re-designating those students as proficient in English," Grimmway is able to go from a student population of about half English language learners to a population of only a quarter of students listed as English learners.

Grimmway Shafter is a new charter school, so its state test scores were not available at the time of the writing of this book. However, the performance of its sister school in Arvin is a good indicator of what to expect in student performance.

In 2015, for example, six out of ten Grimmway Arvin students scored at the proficient level on the state reading assessment and 65 percent scored proficient on the state math test. In 2015, the average student growth in reading and math exceeded one year, while 30 percent of students made one-and-a-half year's growth in math or reading.[29]

The retention rate at Grimmway Arvin has also been high. Since that school was founded in 2011, eight out of ten students have remained enrolled at the Arvin school for all four years.

The most important factor to consider in judging Grimmway Shafter is what parents at the school think. In January and in May, the school surveys parents to get their feedback on the effectiveness of school programs in areas of academics and school culture and climate. The latest 2018 data indicate:

## PARENT SURVEY: *ACADEMICS*

| Curriculum | 98% approval |
|---|---|
| School Choice | 96% |
| Edible School Yard | 95% |
| High Expectations/ High Support | 93% |
| Home Activities (homework) | 65% |
| Extra Curriculars (art, music, PE) | 98% |

## PARENT SURVEY: *SCHOOL CULTURE AND CLIMATE*

| Student Discipline | 84% |
|---|---|
| Café Program | 97% |
| Parent Conferences | 81% |
| Teacher Relationships | 88% |
| Support Staff Relationships | 96% |
| School Leadership | 93% |
| Parent Communication | 90% |

As can be seen in these results, which almost all range between 80 percent to 100 percent approval, parents at Grimmway Academy have a very positive view of the school and the education their children are receiving.

Escala says, "when we see [parents and their children] returning, we see them coming back, we know that ultimately they are satisfied because they don't have to come to us."

The school engages parents in a variety of ways. One of the key ways, according to school leaders, is the commitment parents make to volunteer thirty hours a year at the school. At Grimmway Arvin, 95 percent of parents there complete the thirty-hour commitment.

Students are also surveyed. The school partners with the organization Transform Education and compares responses from students at Grimmway Shafter with Transform Education's cohort norms. The response categories included: curiosity, growth mindset, perseverance, self-awareness, and self-efficacy. In each of these categories, students at Grimmway Shafter gave higher ratings to their school compared to the cohort norm.

The story of Grimmway Academy may seem like just another charter school success story until one realizes that what Grimmway is doing is truly cutting edge: providing a high quality school-choice option to parents and their children in rural America.

The reality is that parents in rural areas across the country often have no choice options other than a regular public school. Charter schools are a primarily urban phenomenon. According to the Brooking Institution, access to charters schools "is highly concentrated among families in urban areas (68 percent have access within ten miles, vs. 17 percent in rural areas)."[30]

The lack of school choice in rural areas ignores the fact that poverty and poor educational attainment are more pronounced in rural communities than the rest of the country. For instance, rural children are more likely to live in poverty than their peers from any other geographic area. Also, only about one in four rural high school graduates go on to college, and just one in five rural adults have a bachelor's degree.[31]

School-choice advocates are starting to realize that they have failed to focus on a huge swath of the America.

Nina Rees, the head of the National Alliance for Public Charter Schools, points out, "Much of our [education reform] movement—whether it advocates for school choice, teacher quality or other initiatives—is focused on urban areas," but as the statistics show, "the educational deficiencies of rural America can be just as stark as those in urban America."[32] Thus, she urges:

> So, without neglecting our essential work in urban America, education reform advocates need to broaden our agenda to include rural America. We have a moral imperative to ensure that students beyond the suburbs have access to a world-class education. We also have a political imperative to broaden the appeal of education reform – it's hard to convince legislators representing rural areas to join our coalition if they believe we are focused exclusively on the needs of cities. A national movement requires national focus.[33]

Rees recommends "creating new schools" in rural America and working to "ensure that every child (regardless of their circumstances) receives customized, personalized instruction that sets them on the path to college or a good career."[34] Grimmway Academy is doing exactly what Rees recommends.

Barbara Grimm-Marshall not only created a new school in the heart of rural California, the Grimmway Academy team is working to create more schools in more rural communities. Further, Grimmway has been a leader in California in implementing a blended-learning instructional model that uses education technology tools to personalize learning for students so that they are put on a trajectory that will vault them eventually into college and a good job.

The bottom line is that Grimmway Shafter is filling a need in a small rural community. Students and parents are very satisfied with what they are receiving from the school. They were given the opportunity to choose a school and they are very happy with their choice. That is success in action. "We want to be an example," says Escala, "and we want to be a choice, but we also want to scale some of the things we do and we want others to learn from us because we want everyone to get better."

Grimmway Academy, therefore, is a pioneer, both in who the school serves and how they are serving them. Indeed, they are a model for charter schools in rural America.

# CHAPTER SIX
## Urban Charters—Controversies from Coast to Coast

*I love interacting with children. Not that I don't like all you and adults, but I would literally choose to spend my time more with children than with grownups. I like them. I like relating to them. I like their uninhibitiveness. I like their questions.*

~ EVA MOSKOWITZ
FOUNDER OF SUCCESS ACADEMY

# Urban Charters—Controversies from Coast to Coast

## MAGNOLIA PUBLIC SCHOOLS

OF ALL CHARTER schools, urban charter schools that serve mostly disadvantaged and/or minority students are probably the most well-known to the public. There are literally thousands of charter schools from which to choose in the urban charter category. For this chapter, however, I chose two charter school networks that have been the target of much controversy, for different reasons, but which parents still strongly support.

I visited Magnolia Science Academy 1 (MSA-1), a charter school serving grades 6-12 in Reseda in Los Angeles' San Fernando Valley. The school is 84 percent Hispanic, 8 percent Asian and 7 percent white. Nine out of ten students are from low-income families. I met Dr. Caprice Young, CEO of the Magnolia Public Schools, under the giant mural of Albert Einstein that covers the entire outer wall next to MSA-1's entrance.

One of California's charter school pioneers, Young was inducted into the National Alliance for Public Charter Schools' Charter School Hall of Fame in 2017.

As we toured MSA-1, we talked about the usual education issues, such as student achievement and different learning programs at MSA-1. But a good chunk of our conversation centered on an eyebrow-raising controversy in which Magnolia is embroiled.

The Magnolia Public Schools is a charter management organization that operates ten charter schools across California that focus on science, technology, engineering, arts, and math (STEAM). Magnolia's schools are located in low-income high-need communities and have won multiple awards and recognitions. For four years in a row, MSA-1 received "Best High School" recognition from *U.S. News & World Report*. All in all, the profile of a successful, but not highly newsworthy, charter school.

Nevertheless, charter schools are not strangers to controversy. School district boards and bureaucrats, plus various special-interest groups, such as teacher unions, have continually stirred the charter pot. However, even among charter tempests, the controversy that has ensnared Magnolia stands out.

Instead of controversy involving intrigue in the state capital, this is intrigue in a capital half a world away. Instead of the involvement of local school board members and state representatives, a U.S. congressman on the House Foreign Affairs Committee became involved. Add in foreign agents, high-powered Washington lobbyists, and efforts of an overseas despot to influence American education decision-making, and you have all the makings of a Netflix mini-series.

The whole brouhaha starts with the fact that several young Turkish Americans founded Magnolia and some of its teachers are Turkish. In a multicultural melting pot like Los Angeles, what should be so controversial about that? A lot, it turns out.

Turkey's president, Recep Tayyip Erdogan, believes that one of his former allies, a Muslim cleric named Fethullah Gulen, who lives in exile in Pennsylvania, was connected to a failed coup against him. The two Turkish-American founders of Magnolia were sympathetic to Gulen and so are some of the Turkish teachers. Sympathetic or not, Caprice Young has stated unequivocally that Magnolia has no legal, financial, or governance connection with Gulen.[1] "Freedom of religion is a core value in the U.S.," she said, and her staff "has that right, but no one brings his or her religion into the workplace."[2]

Yet the *OC Daily*, reported that "The Erdogan regime zeroed in on Magnolia Public Schools as part of a world-wide campaign targeting anything that might be tinged in any way by Gulen."[3]

Dr. Young, who previously served as president of the Los Angeles school board and as CEO of the California Charter School Association, testified at one school board meeting, that Erdogan's attorney, "is telling bald-faced lies intended to hurt the children we serve."[4]

One person who shares Young's perspective is U.S. Representative Brad Sherman (D-CA), the second-ranking Democrat on the House Foreign Affairs Committee. He wrote in a 2016 letter that the Erdogan government's efforts against Magnolia "is a repudiation of everything that good American schools stand for."[5]

Dr. Young told me about how the intervention of Erdogan's agents played out in a battle over the renewal of MSA-1 by the Los Angeles school board. Accusations were made against Magnolia regarding supposed financial mis-management, despite those charges being disproved by the California State Auditor's Office. She told me that one key board member voiced concern that MSA-1 was supposedly dependent on immigration from Turkey, which it was not.

Further, and more shocking, she said, "lobbyists representing the Republic of Turkey met with him one day, then a couple of days later gave him a major contribution, and then a week later he voted against our charter."

"All of the lies," she said, "were disproven again, but it was very clearly an alliance of convenience between [the anti-charter] forces and the Republic of Turkey. You can't make this stuff up."

The Los Angeles school board caved to the pressures of this bizarre coalition and voted against renewing MSA-1. However, the story has a happy ending. Magnolia appealed to the Los Angeles County Board of Education, and the latter simply looked at the objective information on the school's finances and its academic record and approved the renewal.

## Magnolia Charter's STEAM Program

Spy-novel plot notwithstanding, MSA-1 is an example of excellence among urban charter schools. The school's mission statement says that its STEAM program is based on three core values: excellence, innovation, and connection.[6]

The school assesses students to find out their learning needs and styles, which, in turn, helps guide educators in developing their curriculum so that it is personalized and aligned to meet students at their affect level. In addition, the school collects and disaggregates data in order to consistently monitor and measure student growth, as well as provide immediate feedback to improve learning and tailor their program to meet the individual needs of the students.[7]

The online curriculum and real-time assessments allow continuous and individualized pacing as well as flexibility in the number of courses students are offered. The school's system generates reports that show profiles of content and skills that students are learning and tracks their progress. This system is combined with other assessments to provide data to build personalized, realistic, and productive learning plans on a weekly basis for every Magnolia student.[8] MSA-1 uses "inquiry and project-based activities to help students acquire core academic knowledge, problem-solving skills, and critical thinking skills." Among the projects on which students work are "real-life" projects that are "aligned with the curriculum, and provide students with opportunities to work within their home community."[9]

For struggling students, MSA-1 offers free afterschool tutoring. The tutoring occurs in a small-group environment where students can receive personalized attention from their teachers, plus access to added resources needed to complete their assignments. Individual tutoring is also available. If students are low achieving, their attendance at afterschool tutoring will be mandatory. The progress of low achieving students is monitored through a variety of tests with the goal of attaining at least one year's academic progress within the school year.[10]

One unique feature of Magnolia's education program is the use of home visits "to not only improve student and school performance, but also identify and intervene early with low-achieving students." These home visits can also provide "new understanding about students' learning styles," and may "reveal the emotional and social needs and behaviors of students." The school says that it is helpful to know if students react to problems with sadness, anger, or withdrawal. It is through these family visits that teachers "can identify students' latest interests or concerns."[11]

As a STEAM-focused school, MSA-1 employs a number of innovative programs. For example, the school offers a robotics course that uses robotics equipment to explore the relationship between math, science in general and physics specifically, and technology. The goal is to use students' interest in robotics to get students to then pursue STEAM-related fields after graduation.

In the robotics course, students work in small groups in lab experiments, where students will build and test mobile robots:

> Besides using computers so that students can learn to design their own robots, they will also have the opportunity to build their robots

themselves, and will also have the opportunity to write their own algorithms. The computer algorithms written by the students will enable the robots to become autonomous. At the same time, these algorithms will give the students the opportunity to solve potential problems with their designs using mathematics and science.[12]

The student teams will participate in competitions between themselves and with other schools.

MSA-1 also has a partnership with the famed Mount Wilson Observatory. The school piloted the first field trips for fifth to twelfth-grade students to the observatory in its history. The observatory sits on the top of a 5,700-foot peak that is an hour's drive from the school. Beginning in 2015-16, Magnolia became the first K-12 educational organization to have access to what had been an underutilized local resource. [13]

The observatory is home to two large historic telescopes, the Hooker telescope and the Hale telescope, as well as several other important astronomical devices.

While having access to world-class equipment is an advantage, the opportunity for students to work with the observatory's scientists is perhaps the best part of the school's partnership with the facility. The scientists work with students as part of a residency program by incorporating online learning and ongoing collaboration with the classroom teacher to get first-hand experience with professionals in the field.[14]

MSA-1's test scores are at about the state average. What is important to understand, however, is that as a grade six though twelve school, MSA-1 receives the products of the local elementary schools. And what Dr. Young has noticed is that the recent students entering MSA-1 from these regular public elementary schools are coming in at lower levels of learning than what was previously the case. "And I'm not the only charter leader who has identified this," she observed. She believes that the elementary schools are not focusing on the core skills.

This change in the level of learning of incoming students has forced a change in Magnolia's teaching practices. Dr. Young said that schools such as MSA-1 used "to really focus on the critical thinking skills and the conceptual skills" in subjects such as math. Now, however, the school has "had to reintroduce stronger computational skills because we can't assume that the kids come in with the computational skills."

Dr. Young emphasized, "We don't have the luxury to say, oh, well, the student came in to our sixth-grade reading on a second-grade level, so don't blame us." Even if that student is initially performing at the second-grade level, it is the school's responsibility to raise their achievement to the sixth-grade level. "Yes, gotta get them there," she said.

Once at MSA-1, the school does do a good job growing the performance of students. One review organization said that students at MSA-1 make "more academic progress from one grade to the next compared to students at other schools in the state."[15]

Other performance indicators demonstrate why the school has received many local, state and national accolades. In its class of 2018, 100 percent of MSA-1's graduating seniors are attending a college or university. No wonder then that parents are very happy with the school. On its 2018 family survey, 95 percent of parents said that they were satisfied with MSA-1 and would recommend it to other students or parents or educators.[16] One parent, in an online review of the school, said:

> Great school! Highly focused on education. The school provides extra support for the college preparedness. My son is in twelfth grade and he is accepted all the UCs he applied. He decided to go to UC Berkeley. Without school's great support, he will not be able to go there. Robot-

ics club is a great opportunity for the students. I highly recommend this school.[17]

Perhaps one of the greatest indications of the parental satisfaction with MSA-1 has been the outpouring of support from families during the renewal fight at the Los Angeles school board meetings. Caprice Young recalled, "We had more than 500 kids and parents and staff come for that renewal, and they made speeches and supported each other in the speeches they were making."

Families also signed a letter that was sent to the Turkish consul general in Los Angeles "demanding the Turkish government stop spending substantial resources on high-powered lobbyists and lawyers to spread false information about their schools in an attempt to shut them down."[18] *The Wall Street Journal* quoted one parent, Lourdes Gonzalez, who said that she was furious that Turkey would meddle in an American school, and emphasized, "We will not allow our children to be used as pawns in a political game taking place 7,000 miles away.[19]

Caprice Young did not mince words when she told me, "I think about charters as putting the public back in public education, and that's exactly contrary to the status quo propaganda." The status quo establishment sees charters "as privatizing when, in fact, it's actually making education more public again because government doesn't control everything." The government controls the output, she observed, "but they don't control the means, and that's really important."

## SUCCESS ACADEMY

Founded in 2006, Success Academy Charter Schools operates forty-seven schools, including elementary, middle, and high schools, serving seventeen thousand students in New

York City, which makes it the largest charter school network in the city. Across the Success Academy network of schools, three-quarters of students are from low-income households and more than nine out of ten are children of color.

Success Academy's stated mission is to build "exceptional, world-class public schools that prove children from all backgrounds can succeed in college and life; and advocate across the country to change public policies that prevent so many from having access to opportunity." The second part of that mission statement is an indicator of why Success Academy has generated so much animosity on the part of anti-charter-school forces.

Success Academy and its founder and leader Eva Moskowitz are not shrinking violets. I personally admire Moskowitz greatly for her fearlessness and willingness to fight, press, and put the record straight about charter schools and many other subjects. It is also probably one of the reasons why, as her quote in the beginning of this chapter indicates, she loves children more than grownups.

Perhaps no other charter-school organization has faced so much controversy as Success Academy. The reasons for these controversies are many, ranging from politics to school policies to personalities.

One of the talking points against Success Academy that is repeated over and over again by the organization's critics is that the Academy's suspension and discipline policies are overly harsh and have the supposed effect of causing harder-to-educate students to leave (attrition), which then improves the Academy's performance figures. This charge is simply untrue. When a reporter for *Education Week* repeated this claim at one of her speaking events, Moskowitz eviscerated him:

> You're stating as facts things that are actually not facts, so just to be really, really clear, our scholar attrition rates are extraordinarily low. Far lower than the

district schools. And suspension, which we do, and we believe that you cannot throw a wooden block at a teacher, and if you do, we are going to suspend you.[20]

Indeed, as Moskowitz pointed out in her memoir, "Network-wide, our attrition rate was 43 percent lower" than the rate at regular New York City public schools.[21] Further, Moskowitz says that the goal of Success Academy is to keep all their students, not to chuck them out. The reasons for this goal are both emotional and pragmatic.

"First, emotionally, we love our kids," she says, "and by the way, love is underestimated as a reform strategy."[22] Second, there is a financial reason, because, "unlike the district school, anytime a kid walks out the door, that's our per-pupil [funding], and we're building our financial model on a certain number of children." Thus, "if that number goes down, that makes it very, very challenging to provide the science five days a week, to provide the dedicated chess teacher, to provide the art and the music and the longer school day because we have to pay our teachers significantly more than the district in order to, you know, run these schools."[23]

Despite all these controversies, however, the bottom line is that Success Academy has lived up to its name and has helped thousands of children, mostly from disadvantaged backgrounds, achieve success in their learning.

In 2018, of the top thirty elementary schools in New York State, based on test calculations by the education research organization SchoolDigger, an amazing seventeen, more than half, are Success Academy charter schools.[24]

Also, a 2017 study by Stanford University's Center for Research on Education Outcomes found that Success Academy students learned much more than students at district public schools. According to *U.S. News & World Report*, the study found that over a three-year period Success Academy students "made 228 more days' worth of math gains than district school students with comparable demographics, as well as 120 more days' worth of gains in reading."[25]

Charles Sahm, a senior fellow at the Manhattan Institute, a New York City based think tank, has extensively studied the Success Academy schools.

In a highly informative article in the scholarly periodical *EducationNext* on Success Academy's undeniable achievements, Sahm asked, "So what's going on?" He answered this question by observing, "What separates Success, in my opinion, is a laser focus on *what* is being taught, and *how*."

In English language arts, Success Academy uses its own curriculum called THINK Literacy, which adheres to the "balanced literacy" theory that emphasizes independent reading. According to Sahm: "THINK Literacy includes Reading Workshop (independent reading and small-group direct instruction); Guided Reading (students read more—challenging books, with help from teachers); Read Aloud (teachers read books aloud, and students discuss the major ideas); and Shared Text (close reading of short texts, emphasizing central meaning and literary techniques)." Each day, he noted, "students spend two hours on some combination of these four components."[26]

Success Academy itself describes the components of its English language arts elementary school curriculum as follows:

> *Independent Reading:* At the heart of our literacy curriculum is sacred Independent Reading time—a time when scholars get lost in books they love. Each classroom is stocked with a generous library of books selected for their rich language and storylines and beautiful illustrations. . . .Through discussions about their books with partners and the whole class, scholars are encouraged to think critically about texts and share in the joy of reading.

*Guided Reading:* In Guided Reading, a teacher works with a small group of scholars who are reading at the same level.... Through close study, coaching, and discussion in a small group setting, scholars are able to master the more challenging content and gain tools to tackle books at this level on their own.

*Shared Poems (GrK-1):* Shared Poem occurs four times a week and consists of reading poems together as a class to develop oral language, phonemic awareness, comprehension, and to enjoy the fun of language.

*Shared Text (Gr2-4):* Together with their teacher, scholars read a one-page poem or text (for example, a fable, short story, or brief biography) in order to understand the author's main idea, or central message. Scholars learn to identify literary techniques and make inferences about the author's meaning.

*Read Aloud:* We build scholars' critical thinking skills and passion for reading by reading aloud rich and engaging books to scholars. Teachers guide scholars to unpack the meaning of the text, think analytically about the author's choices, and discuss and debate the ideas with partners and the whole class.

*Success for All (GrK-1):* ... In daily direct instruction that is fast-paced and engaging, scholars build phonemic awareness and decoding skills that strengthen oral language and build reading fluency and comprehension.... Through this powerful program, kindergarten and first-grade scholars quickly master the foundational reading skills they need to read independently.[27]

In middle school, Sahm found, "Success adds independent reading time and includes a literature class," plus students "receive iPads loaded with books." Middle school students "must read seven key texts, typically comprising four novels, two nonfiction books and one of poetry." On one of his visits, he saw "middle-school students in Harlem reading *The Block*, which combines poetry of Langston Hughes with paintings of Harlem Renaissance artist Romare Beardon."[28]

Sahm noted that Success Academy developed its own math curriculum. He spoke to the Academy's director of math and science, who said teachers "plan the lesson with a clear goal and use precise questioning and a carefully designed set of activities to lead scholars to learn, develop, or master a new concept each day."[29]

Success Academy's math curriculum is constructivist, said Sahm.[30] According to Moskowitz, "our method of pedagogy is unbelievably student-centered and inquiry based." She agrees with John Dewey that "kids learn best by doing."[31] And so, Moskowitz observes, "there's very limited direct instruction," which accounts for "10 minutes a day per subject, and the rest of that is student-led discussion, guided practice, and independent practice."[32]

In elementary school math, Success Academy says that lessons "are centered on tackling complex, multidimensional problems that have correct answers but innumerable ways to arrive at these answers."[33] Using a constructivist approach, students are pushed to think creatively and independently to develop their own approach to solving these problems, "which strengthens their ability to apply prior knowledge to new context and deepens their conceptual understanding."[34]

Sahm observed, "Besides encouraging student-generated strategies to solve math problems, Success devotes considerable effort in the early grades to honing students' arithmetic skills."[35] Indeed, Success Academy says that its math program develops students' computational fluency through daily practice of so-called "math facts."[36] The components of the elementary school math curriculum includes:

*Mini-lessons:* During Mini-lessons, scholars gather on the rug and are asked to solve a series of problems in quick succession and discuss their thinking. This practice develops skills and fluency in counting, number sense, and in concepts such as rounding and telling time.

*Math Workshop:* Math Workshop introduces scholars to new math content in topics such as geometry, fractions, measurement, and data. It also supports conceptual understanding of counting, number sense, and place value. Scholars work together to solve problems, and learn from each other during whole-class discourse.

*Number Stories*: During Number Stories, scholars develop problem-solving skills by independently working to solve unfamiliar, contextualized problems. . . teachers challenge scholars to come up with their own strategies so that they become increasingly flexible mathematical thinkers.

*No Hesitation Math (NMH):* NHM ensures scholars can quickly, accurately, and flexibly solve mental math facts. Scholars begin in first grade with addition and subtraction facts. Beginning in third grade, they expand to multiplication and division.

*Counting Jar:* Counting is the foundation of all math. Counting Jar helps scholars to become fluent with number names, number sequences, and to understand the way in which numbers correspond to objects.

Moskowitz emphasizes the rigor of the Success Academy's math curriculum. She does not think that the Common Core national education standards, which most states have adopted, is a rigorous guide: "we're the only people seemingly in the entire country who think Common Core is too easy."[37] She observes "... it doesn't set kids up for the level of success that they're going to need."[38]

Science is used as a way to really interest children in their learning. Surveying the American education landscape, Moskowitz says, "I actually believe that most kids in America are extremely bored by school." She observes, "It's not terribly engaging and interesting."[39] Success Academy upends the boredom model. "We believed that children have a natural curiosity," says Moskowitz, "so we determined that science was not going to be a second-class subject."[40] "The easiest thing in the world is to get kids interested in science," she notes. "You are not swimming upstream."[41]

Humorously, Moskowitz reminds people: "Why do you think you have to put those safety sockets on the [electrical] outlets, right? Because they want to stick their finger in and see what happens." Schools, she advises, "need to take advantage of that curiosity instead of building a culture where asking a question is not celebrated."[42]

At Success Academy, "in our science class five days a week, we celebrate questioning, as we do in all the other subjects." Unlike most regular public schools where science is only taught a couple of days a week starting in the fourth grade, Moskowitz says that at Success Academy, "We were going to do science every day of the week starting in kindergarten."[43]

"Our kindergarteners do 135 experiments by the end of kindergarten," she says, "and they do that every single year."[44] Success Academy says that its science program "is like none other in the country." Beginning in kindergarten, students receive daily "hands-on, inquiry-based science with a dedicated science teacher." Specifically, in the elementary science curriculum:

Every day, scholars conduct experiments and discuss observations, data, and results in the same way true scientists do. . . .

Science lessons launch with hands-on exploration of a challenge or question presented by the teacher. . . After scholars work collaboratively on the challenge and record their observations, they participate in rich discussion about their discoveries, during which the teacher guides them to a deeper understanding of the scientific principles embedded in the lesson. Finally, scholars write up their conclusions in reports that grow in sophistication over the course of elementary school.[45]

Like other schools that use progressive teaching methodologies, Success Academy makes extensive use of projects to enhance the learning process. "Our scholars," says the Academy, "learn the thrill of becoming experts in a subject through Project-Based Learning (PBL), when they have extended time to immerse themselves in a fascinating topic."[46]

For example, the Academy says that twice a year, students "explore subjects in depth over several weeks from a cross-disciplinary perspective—science, reading, writing, math, and art." Students "work collaboratively to build expertise, develop insights, and apply their knowledge in creative projects." At the close of each unit, "families are invited to classrooms to view PBL museums and performances showcasing scholars' newly gained expertise."[47]

As part of its project-based-learning approach, Success Academy gives students memorable experiences to promote learning. Success Academy makes great use of its location in New York City, arranging field trips for students to visit museums, theaters, circuses, and other notable venues. These field trips number about twenty per year. Students "make connections between classroom learning and the real world and broaden their knowledge and experience."[48]

Contrary to the accusation that Success Academy turns teachers into drones repeating tightly scripted lessons, Sahm observed that Academy teachers "actually spend more time working individually with students than at other schools."[49]

Among the many false knocks against Success Academy is the argument that it is a so-called "test-prep factory" where students are only drilled on math and English so they can do well on state standardized exams. When he toured a Success Academy middle school in Harlem, he said, "that's not what I saw." Rather, he saw just the opposite:

> In one room, the chess team prepared for the national tournament; in another, students worked on the school newspaper; down the hall, students rehearsed a musical; in other rooms, students worked on art projects or learned computer coding. Success's debate and chess teams have begun to win national awards.[50]

Indeed, as opposed to the caricature of Success Academy students as robotic regurgitators of facts and figures, the Academy states explicitly that a great education "consists of more than just rigorous academics." It seeks to educate the "whole child" by providing "numerous opportunities for scholars to explore talents and interests outside of reading, writing, math, and science."[51]

Success Academy schools offer so-called "specials" and electives that include art, chess, sports, and depending on the school, dance, music, or theater. At the elementary level, for instance, students participate in "one special (grades K-2) or elective (grades three and four) for 45 minutes per day." In grades K-2, students rotate through all specials available at the school, while in grades three and four, students select two to study the whole year.[52]

As Sahm noted, chess has a special role at Success Academy. Eva Moskowitz has said that besides rigorous academics, "The other thing about our schools is that there are some 'non-academic' subjects that for us are really part and parcel of what we think of as a great education." So, for example, "all of our kids take chess starting in kindergarten."[53]

"We think games, intellectually stimulating games," she observes, "are really, really good for kids, and I would argue that chess is one of the most powerful games for children."[54] She likes chess because, among other things, it is a non-verbal game. "There are various forms of intelligence," she says, "and what you get when you take the verbal skill off the table is you get this pure, strategic form of thinking," where students "think five, six, seven moves ahead."[55]

"We have an incredible chess culture at our schools," says Moskowitz. "Not only does everyone play chess starting in kindergarten," she says, "but we compete starting in third grade."[56] The school sends multiple teams to both state and national championship tournaments. If students use the timing clock, chess games can last up to four hours.

Moskowitz says that students get so much into chess that "on Saturday they play three games a day, so kids are playing chess for 12 hours."[57] "Their level of concentration and focus is just really, really high," she beams, "and they're building intellectual stamina while having a ball, and that's incredibly important."[58]

### Teacher Training

For all the rigor running through its academic and non-academic curricula, Moskowitz says, "there is one other factor that I think is critical to our success, and that is our training of educators." "The training of educators in this country needs a fundamental revamping," she observes. "People tend to think of the district schools and what needs revamping there," she says, "but the [university] schools of education are not producing graduates who can do the job."[59]

To combat the teacher-training deficiencies of the ed schools, "we have found as a network that we've had to go into teacher training and principal training in order to scale and be successful." Success Academy teachers get thirteen weeks of training every year, and the focus is on content knowledge.[60]

Emphasis on subject-matter knowledge is largely absent in university teacher-training courses. In contrast, according to Moskowitz, Success Academy pushes teachers to have a deep understanding of the subject matter that they are teaching.

"We should not wonder why our kids in the STEM fields are not doing as well," Moskowitz says, "when we don't have content mastery [by teachers] in mathematics and science, particularly at the middle-school level." She notes, "It is a real, real crisis, and so we have found that we have to become a school of education."[61]

Unlike many teacher union collective bargaining contracts, where principals are restricted from making drop-in visits to classrooms to observe teachers in action, school leaders regularly visit classrooms and offer teachers feedback and recommendations.[62]

Sahm observed that Success Academy teachers have a lot of access to technology tools. Also, teachers and leaders share videos of effective and ineffective lessons. "Shortly before a lesson is taught across the network," he observed, "an experienced teacher delivers (and video-records) the lesson early to her students, and shares the recording with other teachers."[63]

All of the teachers with whom he spoke said that Success Academy prepares its teachers well. He quoted one teacher who said, "You know the material at such a high level that it gives you a real confidence in the classroom." Even critical former teachers, he said, credited the Academy with improving their teaching.[64]

Moskowitz also views parental involvement as a crucial component of the Success Academy formula. "It's not only the subjects that you teach," she says, "it's your vision of parental investment."[65] Many schools claim to believe in parental involvement, but actually wall themselves off from parents by "creating schools as fortresses where parents can't get in the building," which "is not going to lead to particularly high levels of parental investment."[66] "At our schools," she points out, "any parent can come into the school and sit in the back of the classroom at any time without an appointment and see what's going on in the school."[67]

Sahm noted that Success Academy teachers "spend much time on parental engagement, via e-mail, phone calls, and meetings." One parent of two Academy students told him that her child never had homework at the district school she attended and that she "had to chase the teachers around to get a meeting." In contrast, at the Academy, "she meets with her daughters' teachers regularly, reviewing their action plan."[68] Further, says Moskowitz, "We encourage a high level of parental investment when it comes to advocacy." Underscoring Success Academy's mission statement that includes an advocacy component, she says, "We bring a tremendous number of parents to Albany to really fight for their right to a great, free public education."[69]

Parent satisfaction rates on surveys are extremely high. Moskowitz has noted, "that not *one single parent* in our entire school selected 'teaching' as something that needed improvement."[70] Also, in 2017, Success Academy had seventeen thousand applicants for three thousand spots.[71]

Looking at the big picture, Moskowitz wonders aloud about why it is that Success Academy that is so controversial rather than the failing regular public schools:

> In New York City, we have a quarter of the schools where more than 90 percent of the kids can't read, write, or do math, and there's an obvious solution, and yet we're constantly being tarred and feathered. It's sort of an odd thing. You would think someone would be rolling out the red carpet, not because we are "the" answer, but we are one of the answers to this profound

crisis, and yet we have to fight on every front to get space, to get funding, to insert ourselves into the public narrative about charters.[72]

Motivated by ideology and raw self-interest, and enjoying powerful political advantages, the anti-charter forces in New York City and across America will never roll out the red carpet for charters like Success Academy, no matter how successful they are. Indeed, the more successful such charter organizations are, the more pushback they will receive—an inverse relationship that is played all over the country, over and over again.

That is why, in my view, we need strong, resolute and fearless charter-school leaders like Eva Moskowitz. We need leaders like her who are willing to go toe-to-toe, mano-y-mano against the powerful forces fighting charter schools. We need leaders like Moskowitz who are willing to risk controversy in order to battle for her schools, her students, and the charter ideal. We need leaders who are willing to fight, not those who shrink at the prospect of confrontation.

Eva Moskowitz is a fighter. Thank God.

# CHAPTER SEVEN
## Successful Urban Schools

"*There are many ways to provide excellent education, but I think the reason we don't universally have excellent education has much more to do with politics than not knowing what would be good for kids and teaching.*

~EVA MOSKOWITZ
FOUNDER OF SUCCESS ACADEMY

# Successful Urban Schools

## AVONDALE MEADOWS ACADEMY

WHILE THE TWO charter-school organizations that I chose to profile in Chapter Six on urban charter schools, Magnolia Public Schools and Success Academy, are noted for both their controversies as well as their successes, it must be stated that there are many charter schools in urban areas around the country that do an excellent job educating students.

Take, for example, the Avondale Meadows Academy (AMA) in Indianapolis, Indiana. Opened in 2006, the same year that Success Academy opened its doors, AMA was part of a network of charter schools started by the Portland, Oregon-based Challenge Foundation. AMA's mission statement says that the school provides "a rigorous and relevant college-preparatory program, grounded in our belief in the ability of every child to succeed at high levels."[1]

United Schools of Indianapolis now operates AMA elementary school and AMA middle school in a low-income, mainly African American, part of Indianapolis. Ninety-five percent of the elementary school's students are African American.

Kelly Herron, the now executive director of United Schools of Indianapolis, has said, "The majority of students come to us below grade level, have little preschool experience and low exposure to reading and language during their early years."[2]

"We have to work hard to close the gap early," she explained, and, "We do so by providing two full-time licensed teachers in every kindergarten classroom." Also, "Small group and differentiated instruction is utilized as much as possible to meet the needs of all learners."[3]

At the elementary school, AMA uses the Core Knowledge curriculum, which provides a broad base of knowledge and vocabulary needed for reading achievement and academic success. The school says, "According to E.D. Hirsch, Jr., author and founder of the Core Knowledge curriculum upon which our school is founded, for the sake of academic excellence, greater fairness, and higher literacy, early schooling should provide a solid, specific, shared, and sequential core curriculum."[4] AMA's Core Knowledge program consists of three Cs:

1. Coherent – Identification of what children should learn at each grade level ensures a coherent approach to building knowledge across all grade levels.

2. Cumulative – Core Knowledge provides a clear outline of content to be learned grade by grade so that knowledge, language, and skills build cumulatively from year to year. This sequential building of knowledge not only helps ensure that children enter each new grade ready to learn, it also helps prevent the repetitions and gaps that so often characterize current education.

3. Content-Specific – Core Knowledge clearly specifies the important knowledge in language arts, history, geography, math, science, and the fine arts.[5]

AMA also uses Benchmark Literacy, which is a comprehensive, research-proven reading and writing program that
focuses on foundational skills. Students build skills in phonics, word study, and fluency to become proficient readers,
and are provided texts at their individual reading level so
that all students are provided the opportunity to grow.[6] After Benchmark Literacy mini-lessons, reader's workshops
take place:

> Students engage in a variety of literacy-based
> activities independently while the teacher meets
> with a small group. The activities are focused
> on comprehension, grammar, and vocabulary.
> In the teacher lead guided reading group, stu-
> dents are reading texts and practicing skills that
> are at their instructional level. These leveled
> groups are designed to meet a variety of learners
> at their different levels.[7]

Kelly Heron has pointed out that the biggest challenges facing her community are generations of poverty and the crime
in the surrounding neighborhoods.[8] Thus, AMA emphasizes a structured culture for the school and its students:

> At Avondale Meadows Academy we believe that
> every child deserves to learn in a safe, positive
> environment. Scholars cannot learn, and teach-
> ers cannot teach in chaos. Therefore, in our
> structured environment, adults are consistently
> positive, yet firm so that scholars are learning in
> a happy and focused school setting. This posi-
> tive and firm approach nurtures a culture with-
> in our school and within each classroom where
> scholars have the confidence to take academic
> risks and learn from their mistakes. Utilizing
> the Culture Rubric developed by AMA, we plan

to build and maintain this culture that reinforces positive behaviors and focuses on academics.[9]

When AMA first started out, it was one of the lowest performing schools in Indiana. Now, in 2017, nearly nine out of 10 elementary students scored at the proficient level on the state reading test, and 65 percent scored at the proficient level on the state math test.[10]

## DSST PUBLIC SCHOOLS

Another charter organization that is meeting the needs of urban students is DSST Public Schools in Denver. With eight middle schools and six high schools in metropolitan Denver, DSST serves a predominantly low-income minority student population—seven out of ten students are low-income, and 83 percent are non-white.

For ten years in a row, 100 percent of DSST graduates have been accepted to a 4-year college or university. DSST runs four out of the top five middle schools in Denver and five of the top eight high schools.

DSST charters have a STEM focus and have a mission to "transform urban public education by eliminating educational iniquity and preparing all students for success in college and the 21st Century."[11]

The schools' core values include: respect, responsibility, integrity, courage, curiosity, and doing your best.

How is it that DSST succeeds in having an unheard of 100-percent college-acceptance rate for a decade? According to the DSST:

> In addition to four years of rigorous academic curriculum, the schools engage students in the exploration of college options through the advisory College Success curriculum and College Planning Seminar classes at all grade levels,

culminating in a required Senior College Seminar class in senior year to support students as they apply for college admission and financial aid. Students participate in required college field trips to Colorado college campuses at all grade levels. All college planning curriculum, activities, and support of students applying to colleges and universities and for financial aid is aligned with the National Association of College Admission Counselors (NACAC) Best Practices.[12]

Given the success of DSST, it is heartening that the charter network plans to expand significantly over the coming years. The goal is for the network to grow from fourteen schools to twenty-two, and from five thousand seven hundred students to ten thousand five hundred students.

In 2018, DSST won the prestigious Broad Prize for Public Charter Schools, which was won by Success Academy in 2017.

Macke Raymond, director of the Center for Research on Education Outcomes at Stanford University, who served as judge for the Broad Prize, said, "DSST is a great example of the much-desired and elusive combination: a network that ensures outstanding results for all types of students while growing to serve more students."[13]

# CONCLUSION

# Conclusion

THE SCHOOLS IN this book demonstrate the incredible diversity of missions, goals, and learning programs in the charter sector. It is hard to imagine, for example, two schools that have more differing teaching and learning philosophies than Design Tech and Mason Classical Academy. And while Mia, one of the students I interviewed at Design Tech, said that her school was perfect for her, the students with whom I spoke at John Adams Academy said that they loved their school.

The reaction of these students is not surprising since, as Eva Moskowitz says, there are many ways to provide excellent education to children. Whether it is NYC Autism Charter School providing a unique education program for children with autism, or Natomas Charter School providing a high quality education with an emphasis on performing and fine arts, the schools profiled in this book are meeting the needs, desires and wants of a wide array of students and their parents.

"I didn't create Success Academies for poor children or for black children or for Latino children," says Moskowitz, "I wanted to create the most magical schooling environment for kids."[1] All of the schools in this book would no doubt agree with her, but they have all gone about doing so in their own very unique ways.

And that is the secret of charter schools—their ability to use the autonomy granted to them to create education programs that are very different from the regular public schools and very different from each other, but which respond to the individual demands of families. No one has to go to a charter school, but parents and their children vote with their feet because, as Moskowitz says, "There's a problem with the system and what's it's delivering for children."[2]

Yet, as Moskowitz also observed, politics stands in the way of making charter-school excellence available to all children in America. Norman Gonzales at John Adams Academy warned that every year the California legislature "is passing new laws that chip away at charter freedom and autonomy" and "they're rolling out additional legislation that says you must teach this, you must do that, they're adding mandates every step of the way."

The question, then, is whether in the future parents will be choosing diversity when they are choosing charter schools, or will they be choosing more conformity. Will those schools be allowed to continue to innovate and create, in the words of Design Tech student Thomas, a "new constantly evolving charter school"? Or, will the forces of the traditional public education status quo succeed, as Norman Gonzales warned, in making charter schools "look as close to them as they can"?

Parents must have the ability to choose diversity when deciding between schools because choice without a difference is no choice at all.

# ENDNOTES

# Introduction

1    California Charter School Association, "What are Charter Schools?," available at http://www.ccsa.org/understanding/what-are-charter-schools.html

2    California Education Code Section 47601(a)-(g)

3    Lindsey Burke, "Why It's OK for This School Choice Program to Underperform on Standardized Tests," *The Daily Signal*, Heritage Foundation, May 30, 2018, available at https://www.heritage.org/education/commentary/why-its-ok-school-choice-program-underperform-standardized-tests

4    Steve Rasmussen, "Why the Smarter Balance Common Core Math Test is Fatally Flawed, *EdSurge*, March 11, 2015, available at https://www.edsurge.com/news/2015-03-11-why-the-smarter-balanced-common-core-math-test-is-fatally-flawed

5    Williamson Evers and Ze'ev Wurman, "California Flies Blind on Testing: The Troubling Saga of the State's 'Smarter Balanced Test,'" *Defining Ideas*, Hoover Institution, Stanford University, August 28, 2018, available at https://www.hoover.org/research/troubling-saga-smarter-balanced-test

6    Williamson Evers and Ze'ev Wurman, "California Flies Blind on Testing: The Troubling Saga of the State's 'Smarter Balanced Test,'" *Defining Ideas*, Hoover Institution, Stanford University, August 28, 2018, available at https://www.hoover.org/research/troubling-saga-smarter-balanced-test

# Chapter 1

1   Ildi Laczko-Derr and Eillen Sigmund, "Myth Busted: Public Charter Schools Do Not 'Cream' District Students," Arizona Charter School Association, August 15, 2018, available at https://azcharters.org/myth-busted-public-charter-schools-do-not-cream-district-students/

2   See http://www.lifelearningacademysf.org

3   Ibid.

4   Ibid.

5   "Charter Renewal Petition," Life Learning Academy, February 2014, p. 3.

6   Ibid, p. 6.

7   Ibid, p. 7.

8   Ibid, p. 8.

9   Ibid, p. 11.

10  Ibid, p. 13.

11  "Charter Renewal Petition," Life Learning Academy, February 2014, p. 13.

12  See http://www.lifelearningacademysf.org

13  "Autism Now: Julie Fisher Extended Interview," April 21, 2011, available at https://www.pbs.org/newshour/show/autism-now-julie-fisher-extended-interview

14  Fran Smith, "Parents Take Over: Two Moms Make a Difference for Autistic Kids," Edutopia, March 19, 2008, available at https://www.edutopia.org/autism-charter-school-parents

15  "Autism Now: Julie Fisher Extended Interview," *PBS NewsHour*, April 21, 2011, available at https://www.pbs.org/newshour/show/autism-now-julie-fisher-extended-interview

16  "SUNY Charter School Institute Proposal and Transmittal and Summary Form [for NYC Autism Charter School Bronx]," SUNY Charter Schools Institute, January 14, 2016, p. 3, available at http://www.newyorkcharters.org/wp-content/uploads/NYCACS-Original-Proposal-Part-1_Redacted.pdf

17  Ibid.

18  See https://www.cdc.gov/ncbddd/autism/data.html

19  Ibid.

20  "SUNY Charter School Institute Proposal and Transmittal and Summary Form [for NYC Autism Charter School Bronx]," SUNY Charter Schools Institute, January 14, 2016, p. 02-1, available at http://www.newyorkcharters.org/wp-content/uploads/NYCACS-Original-Proposal-Part-1_Redacted.pdf

21  Ibid, pp. 02-1-02-2.

22  Ibid, p. 02-2.

23  Ibid.

24  Ibid.

25  Ibid.

26 "Autism Now: Julie Fisher Extended Interview," *PBS NewsHour*, April 21, 2011, available at https://www.pbs.org/newshour/show/autism-now-julie-fisher-extended-interview

27 Ibid, p. 02-4.

28 Robin Lake, "NYC Autism Charter School Solves for Complex Learners With Intense Dedication & Commitment—Personalized Learning at Its Best," *The 74*, August 3, 2018, available at https://www.the74million.org/article/robin-lake-nyc-autism-charter-school-solves-for-complex-learners-with-intense-dedication-commitment-personalized-learning-at-its-best/

29 Ibid.

30 Ibid.

31 Ibid.

32 Ibid.

33 Ibid.

34 Ibid.

35 Ibid.

36 Ibid.

37 Ibid.

38 Robin Lake, "NYC Autism Charter School Solves for Complex Learners With Intense Dedication & Commitment—Personalized Learning at Its Best," *The 74*, August 3, 2018, available at https://www.the74million.org/article/robin-lake-nyc-autism-charter-school-solves-for-complex-learners-with-intense-dedication-commitment-personalized-learning-at-its-best/

39   Ibid.

40   Ibid.

41   Eliza Shapiro, "A charter school models how the city
     can educate autistic children, *Politico*, October 30,
     2017, available at https://www.politico.com/states/
     new-york/city-hall/story/2017/10/30/in-harlem-
     and-the-bronx-a-charter-school-models-how-the-
     city-can-educate-autistic-children-115314

42   Ibid.

43   Ibid.

44   Julie Fisher, "NYC Autism School wow parents,
     teachers and community at holiday concert," Walton
     Family Foundation, December 21, 2016, available
     at https://www.waltonfamilyfoundation.org/stories/
     julie-fisher

45   Ibid.

46   "Autism Now: Julie Fisher Extended Interview," *PBS
     NewsHour*, April 21, 2011, available at https://www.
     pbs.org/newshour/show/autism-now-julie-fisher-
     extended-interview

47   Robin Lake, "NYC Autism Charter School Solves
     for Complex Learners With Intense Dedication &
     Commitment—Personalized Learning at Its Best,"
     *The 74*, August 3, 2018, available at https://www.
     the74million.org/article/robin-lake-nyc-autism-
     charter-school-solves-for-complex-learners-with-
     intense-dedication-commitment-personalized-
     learning-at-its-best/

48 "Autism Now: Julie Fisher Extended Interview," *PBS NewsHour*, April 21, 2011, available at https://www.pbs.org/newshour/show/autism-now-julie-fisher-extended-interview

49 Eliza Shapiro, "A charter school models how the city can educate autistic children, *Politico*, October 30, 2017, available at https://www.politico.com/states/new-york/city-hall/story/2017/10/30/in-harlem-and-the-bronx-a-charter-school-models-how-the-city-can-educate-autistic-children-115314

50 Ibid.

51 Robin Lake, "NYC Autism Charter School Solves for Complex Learners With Intense Dedication & Commitment—Personalized Learning at Its Best," *The 74*, August 3, 2018, available at https://www.the74million.org/article/robin-lake-nyc-autism-charter-school-solves-for-complex-learners-with-intense-dedication-commitment-personalized-learning-at-its-best/

52 Eliza Shapiro, "A charter school models how the city can educate autistic children, *Politico*, October 30, 2017, available at https://www.politico.com/states/new-york/city-hall/story/2017/10/30/in-harlem-and-the-bronx-a-charter-school-models-how-the-city-can-educate-autistic-children-115314

53 Ibid.

54 "Autism Now: Julie Fisher Extended Interview," *PBS NewsHour*, April 21, 2011, available at https://www.pbs.org/newshour/show/autism-now-julie-fisher-extended-interview

55　Eliza Shapiro, "A charter school models how the city can educate autistic children, *Politico*, October 30, 2017, available at https://www.politico.com/states/new-york/city-hall/story/2017/10/30/in-harlem-and-the-bronx-a-charter-school-models-how-the-city-can-educate-autistic-children-115314

56　Julie Fisher, "NYC Autism School wow parents, teachers and community at holiday concert," Walton Family Foundation, December 21, 2016, available at https://www.waltonfamilyfoundation.org/stories/julie-fisher

## Chapter 2

1　"Performing and Fine Arts Academy (PFAA)," Natomas Charter School, available at http://pfaa.natomascharter.org

2　Ibid.

3　"Student and Parent Handbook 2018-19 School Year," Natomas Charter School Performing and Fine Arts Academy, p. 6, available at https://docs.google.com/document/d/1W8rsTV2JXkwAzVuwVy8Bj-DhpHL_r6JC0sdNDqUjPC8/edit#heading=h.ip1ubftdy1xl

4　Ibid.

5　"Pursuing Academic Choices Together (PACT)," Natomas Charter School, see http://pact.natomascharter.org/

6　Ibid.

7　"Virtual Learning Academy (VLA)," Natomas Charter School, see http://vla.natomascharter.org

8    Ibid.

9    "Star Academy," Natomas Charter School, see http://star.natomascharter.org/

10   See https://classicalacademy.com/about/executive-directors-message/

11   Ibid.

12   Ibid.

13   "Charter Renewal Petition," The Classical Academy, submitted to Escondido Union School District, 2014, p. 8.

14   "Charter Document," Classical Academy High School, submitted to Escondido Union High School District, April 15, 2015, p. 4.

15   "Charter Renewal Petition," The Classical Academy, submitted to Escondido Union School District, 2014, p. 4.

## Chapter 3

1    Ibid, p. 14.

2    Ibid.

3    Ibid, p. 18.

4    Ibid, p. 14.

5    Ibid, p. 15.

6    See http://www.designtechhighschool.org/general-academics-1/

7   "Charter Petition" (revised version)," Design Tech High School, November 16, 2017, p. 15.

8   Ibid.

9   "Charter Petition" (revised version)," Design Tech High School, November 16, 2017, p. 18.

10  Ibid, p. 15.

11  Ibid, p. 20.

12  Ibid, p. 11.

13  http://www.designtechhighschool.org/stem-1/

14  See https://www.greatschools.org/california/burlingame/32204-Design-Tech-High/

15  Kaylene Williams and Caroline Williams, "Five key ingredients for improving student motivation," *Research in Higher Education Journal*, p. 2, available at http://www.aabri.com/manuscripts/11834.pdf

16  Ibid., p. 18.

17  "The Science of Summit," Summit Public Schools, 2017, p. 11, available at https://cdn.summitlearning.org/assets/marketing/The-Science-of-Summit-by-Summit-Public-Schools_08072017.pdf

18  Ibid, p. 15.

19  Ibid, p. 37.

20  "Student Handbook," Summit Shasta Public School, 2018-19, p. 9, available at https://docs.google.com/document/d/1Fzf9jLz4PoQD-eP1wIchPCGbJY118yUHwET9RwI_810/edit

21  "The Science of Summit," Summit Public Schools, 2017, p. 42, available at https://cdn.summitlearning. org/assets/marketing/The-Science-of-Summit-by-Summit-Public-Schools_08072017.pdf

22  "Student Handbook," Summit Shasta Public School, 2018-19, p. 9, available at https://docs. google.com/document/d/1Fzf9jLz4PoQD-eP1wIchPCGbJY118yUHwET9RwI_810/edit

23  Ibid, p. 39.

24  Ibid, p. 9.

25  Ibid.

26  Ibid, p. 11.

27  "The Science of Summit," Summit Public Schools, 2017, p. 43, available at https://cdn.summitlearning. org/assets/marketing/The-Science-of-Summit-by-Summit-Public-Schools_08072017.pdf

28  Ibid, p. 38.

29  Ibid, pp. 30-34.

30  "Student Handbook," Summit Shasta Public School, 2018-19, p. 9, available at https://docs. google.com/document/d/1Fzf9jLz4PoQD-eP1wIchPCGbJY118yUHwET9RwI_810/edit

31  "The Science of Summit," Summit Public Schools, 2017, p. 34, available at https://cdn.summitlearning. org/assets/marketing/The-Science-of-Summit-by-Summit-Public-Schools_08072017.pdf

32  Ibid, p. 33.

33  "Student Handbook," Summit Shasta Public School, 2018-19, p. 35, available at https://docs.google.com/document/d/1Fzf9jLz4PoQD-eP1wIchPCGbJY118yUHwET9RwI_810/edit

34  Ibid, p. 10.

35  Ibid, p. 61.

36  Ibid, p. 62.

37  "Summit Learning," available at summitlearning.org

38  Ibid, p. 63.

39  Ibid.

40  Ibid, pp. 64-65.

41  Student Handbook," Summit Shasta Public School, 2018-19, p. 18, available at https://docs.google.com/document/d/1Fzf9jLz4PoQD-eP1wIchPCGbJY118yUHwET9RwI_810/edit

42  Ibid.

43  Ibid, p. 26.

44  Ibid.

45  See https://www.greatschools.org/california/daly-city/31109-Summit-Public-School-Shasta/

46  See http://shasta.summitps.org

47  Ibid.

48  David Osborne, "Schools of the Future: California's Summit Public Schools," Progressive Policy Institute, January 2016, p. 15, available at https://www.progressivepolicy.org/wp-content/uploads/2016/01/2016.01-Osborne_Schools-of-the-Future_Californias-Summit-Public-Schools.pdf

49   "Summit Public Schools Build on History of
     Graduation Success, with 99 Percent of Students
     Accepted to College," Summit Public Schools, June
     8, 2017, available at http://www.summitps.org/
     uploads/images/news/SummitGraduation2017-
     GeneralPRFINAL.pdf

50   Ibid.

51   David Osborne, "Schools of the Future:
     California's Summit Public Schools," Progressive
     Policy Institute, January 2016, p. 14, available at
     https://www.progressivepolicy.org/wp-content/
     uploads/2016/01/2016.01-Osborne_Schools-of-the-
     Future_Californias-Summit-Public-Schools.pdf

52   Michael Horn, "When It Comes to Blended Learning,
     Charter Schools Get Most of the Attention,"
     *Education Next* blog, June 1, 2015, available at http://
     educationnext.org/when-it-comes-to-blended-learning-
     charter-schools-get-most-of-the-attention/

53   Ibid.

## Chapter 4

1   See https://www.johnadamsacademy.org/apps/pages/
    index.jsp?uREC_ID=297377&type=d&pREC_
    ID=685974

2   https://www.johnadamsacademy.org/apps/pages/
    index.jsp?uREC_ID=802493&type=d&pREC_
    ID=1325446

3   Ibid.

4    See https://www.johnadamsacademy.org/apps/pages/
index.jsp?uREC_ID=297377&type=d&pREC_
ID=688443

5    See https://www.johnadamsacademy.org/apps/pages/
index.jsp?uREC_ID=297377&type=d&pREC_
ID=688444

6    https://www.johnadamsacademy.org/apps/pages/
index.jsp?uREC_ID=297377&type=d&pREC_
ID=702463

7    Ibid.

8    Ibid.

9    "John Adams Academy—El Dorado Hills Charter
School Petition," John Adams Academy, February
2018, p. 36.

10   Ibid, p. 38.

11   Ibid, p. 44.

12   Ibid, p. 26.

13   Ibid, pp. 26-27.

14   See https://www.johnadamsacademy.org/apps/pages/
index.jsp?uREC_ID=802493&type=d&pREC_
ID=1332382

15   Ibid.

16   Ibid.

17   Ibid.

18   See https://www.johnadamsacademy.org/apps/pages/
index.jsp?uREC_ID=297377&type=d&pREC_
ID=688443

19  See https://www.johnadamsacademy.org/apps/pages/
    index.jsp?uREC_ID=1316599&type=d&pREC_
    ID=1516042

20  "John Adams Academy—El Dorado Hills Charter
    School Petition," John Adams Academy, February
    2018, p. 51.

21  Ibid.

22  Ibid.

23  Ibid.

24  Ibid, p. 29.

25  Ibid, p. 30.

26  See https://docs.google.com/forms/d/1L2av5mur
    AjyoXYTGRg0IRc9dAkK539Fy5VJmjwtKxoQ/
    edit#responses

27  Ibid.

28  Ibid.

29  See https://www.hillsdale.edu/educational-outreach/
    barney-charter-school-initiative/

30  See video embedded in https://www.hillsdale.edu/
    educational-outreach/barney-charter-school-initiative/

31  See https://masonclassicalacademy.org/apps/pages/
    index.jsp?uREC_ID=223870&type=d&termREC_
    ID=&pREC_ID=436402

32  Terrance Moore, "A Classical Education for Modern
    Times," available at https://masonclassicalacademy.
    org/apps/pages/index.jsp?uREC_
    ID=223870&type=d&termREC_ID=&pREC_
    ID=515244

33   Ibid.

34   See https://masonclassicalacademy.org/apps/pages/
     index.jsp?uREC_ID=224399&type=d&termREC_
     ID=&pREC_ID=553584

35   See https://www.greatschools.org/florida/
     naples/18608-Mason-Classical-Academy/

36   Ibid.

37   See https://masonclassicalacademy.org/apps/pages/
     index.jsp?uREC_ID=223870&type=d&termREC_
     ID=&pREC_ID=515249

38   See https://www.greatschools.org/florida/
     naples/18608-Mason-Classical-Academy/

39   Ibid.

40   Ibid.

41   Ibid.

42   See https://masonclassicalacademy.org/apps/pages/
     index.jsp?uREC_ID=223870&type=d&termREC_
     ID=&pREC_ID=515247

43   Ibid.

44   Ibid.

45   Ibid.

46   See https://www.greatschools.org/florida/
     naples/18608-Mason-Classical-Academy/

47   Ibid.

48   Ibid.

49  Jeanne Chall, *The Academic Achievement Challenge* (New York: The Guilford Press, 2000): p. 171. For a discussion of different teaching methodologies and the empirical evidence supporting them, see Lance Izumi and K. Gwynne Coburn, "Facing the Classroom Challenge," Pacific Research Institute, April 2001, available at https://files.eric.ed.gov/fulltext/ED456094.pdf

50  Ibid, p. 58.

51  See https://masonclassicalacademy.org/apps/pages/index.jsp?uREC_ID=224618&type=d&termREC_ID=&pREC_ID=439159

52  See https://www.greatschools.org/florida/naples/18608-Mason-Classical-Academy/

53  See video embedded in https://www.hillsdale.edu/educational-outreach/barney-charter-school-initiative/

54  Ibid.

## Chapter 5

1  See https://www.gashafter.org

2  Ibid.

3  Ibid.

4  Ibid, p. 10.

5  Ibid.

6  Ibid, p. 11.

7  Ibid.

8	Grimmway Academy Shafter, "Charter Petition," 2017, p. 9.

9	Ibid, p. 34.

10	Ibid, p. 35.

11	Ibid.

12	Timothy Shanahan, "Can I Still Rely on the National Reading Panel Report?," *Reading Rockets*. August 22, 2017, available at http://shanahanonliteracy.com/blog/can-i-still-rely-on-the-national-reading-panel-report#sthash.Zv59KhV3.dpbs

13	Ibid.

14	Ibid.

15	Ibid, p. 44.

16	Ibid.

17	Ibid, p. 37.

18	Ibid. The school notes that while NWREL 6 gives teachers a solid foundation and successful model of instruction for writing, it also gives teachers other writing strategies, including Step Up to Writing and Lucy Calkin's Units of Study. Step Up to Writing provides models and strategies to help students organize their ideas prior to generating writing, is helpful to new and beginning teachers, and helps English learners "to better prepare for the task of producing organized and effective writing." The Lucy Calking's Units of Study focus on specific strategies and elements of strong writing, such as idea generation.

19	Ibid, p. 38.

20	Ibid, p. 39.

21 Barak Rosenshine and Robert Stevens, "Teaching Functions," in *Handbook on Research on Teaching*, Merlin Wittrock, ed. (New York, NY: Macmillan, 1986), p. 378.

22 Grimmway Academy Shafter, "Charter Petition," 2017, p. 38.

23 Ibid.

24 Ibid, p. 50.

25 Ibid.

26 Ibid, p. 49.

27 Ibid.

28 Ibid.

29 Ibid, p. 11.

30 Matthew Chingos and Kristin Blagg, "Who would benefit from school choice? Mapping access to public and private schools," Brookings Institution, March 31, 2017, available at https://www.brookings.edu/research/who-could-benefit-from-school-choice-mapping-access-to-public-and-private-schools/

31 Nina Rees, "The Rural School Reform Opportunity," *U.S. News & World Report,* January 26, 2018, available at https://www.usnews.com/opinion/knowledge-bank/articles/2018-01-26/rural-students-deserve-education-reform-and-school-choice-too

32 Ibid.

33 Ibid.

34 Ibid.

# Chapter 6

1    Ibid.

2    "Ankara to Anaheim: Moreno Dodges Commenting on Alliance with Repressive Turkish Regime," *OC Daily*, May 13, 2016, available at http://www.ocdaily. net/home/ankara-to-anaheim-moreno-dodges-commenting-on-alliance-with-repressive-turkish-regime/

3    Ibid.

4    "Turkey's Battle With Muslim Cleric Careens Through U.S. Classrooms," *The Wall Street Journal*, September 22, 2016, available at https://www.wsj.com/ articles/turkeys-battle-with-muslim-cleric-careens-through-u-s-classrooms-1474553432

5    Ibid.

6    "Charter School Renewal Petition for a Five-Year Term (July 1, 2017-June 30, 2022), Magnolia Public Schools, submitted to the Los Angeles County Board of Education on November 4, 2016.

7    Ibid, p. 30.

8    Ibid, p. 45.

9    Ibid, pp. 30-31.

10   Ibid, p. 46.

11   Ibid, p. 48.

12   Ibid, p. 73.

13   Ibid, p. 53.

14    Ibid.

15    See https://www.greatschools.org/california/
      reseda/12281-Magnolia-Science-Academy/

16    "2017-18 School Year Stakeholder Survey Reflections,"
      Magnolia Science Academy-1, available upon request.

17    See https://www.greatschools.org/california/
      reseda/12281-Magnolia-Science-Academy/

18    "Turkey's Battle With Muslim Cleric Careens
      Through U.S. Classrooms," *The Wall Street Journal*,
      September 22, 2016, available at https://www.wsj.com/
      articles/turkeys-battle-with-muslim-cleric-careens-
      through-u-s-classrooms-1474553432

19    Ibid.

20    Ibid, p. 16.

21    Eva Moskowitz, *The Education of Eva Moskowitz* (New
      York, NY: Harper Collins, 2017), p. 318.

22    "Setting a New Standard for Success in
      Education," The Brookings Institution/Carnegie
      Endowment, September 9, 2015, p. 17, available
      at https://www.brookings.edu/wp-content/
      uploads/2015/08/20150909_success_education_
      transcript.pdf

23    Ibid.

24    See https://www.schooldigger.com/go/NY/
      schoolrank.aspx

25    "Innovating Education," *U.S. News & World Report*,
      November 14, 2017, available athttps://www.usnews.
      com/news/the-report/articles/2017-11-14/success-
      academy-charter-schools-aim-to-innovate-education

26 Charles Sahm, "What Explains the Success at Success Academy?," *Education Next*, Summer 2015, available at https://www.educationnext.org/what-explains-success-academy-charter-network/

27 "The Elementary School Curriculum," Success Academy, 2018-19, pp. 5-6, available at https://www.successacademies.org/app/uploads/2018/05/es-curriculum-guide.pdf

28 Charles Sahm, "What Explains the Success at Success Academy?," *Education Next*, Summer 2015, available at https://www.educationnext.org/what-explains-success-academy-charter-network/

29 Ibid.

30 Ibid.

31 "Setting a New Standard for Success in Education," The Brookings Institution/Carnegie Endowment, September 9, 2015, p. 6, available at https://www.brookings.edu/wp-content/uploads/2015/08/20150909_success_education_transcript.pdf

32 Ibid.

33 "The Elementary School Curriculum," Success Academy, 2018-19, p. 8, available at https://www.successacademies.org/app/uploads/2018/05/es-curriculum-guide.pdf

34 Ibid.

35 Charles Sahm, "What Explains the Success at Success Academy?," *Education Next*, Summer 2015, available at https://www.educationnext.org/what-explains-success-academy-charter-network/

36  "The Elementary School Curriculum," Success Academy, 2018-19, p. 8, available at https://www.successacademies.org/app/uploads/2018/05/es-curriculum-guide.pdf

37  "Setting a New Standard for Success in Education," The Brookings Institution/Carnegie Endowment, September 9, 2015, p. 6, available at https://www.brookings.edu/wp-content/uploads/2015/08/20150909_success_education_transcript.pdf

38  Ibid.

39  Ibid, p. 4.

40  Ibid.

41  Ibid.

42  Ibid.

43  Ibid.

44  Ibid.

45  "The Elementary School Curriculum," Success Academy, 2018-19, p. 10, available at https://www.successacademies.org/app/uploads/2018/05/es-curriculum-guide.pdf

46  Ibid, p. 12.

47  Ibid.

48  Ibid, p. 13.

49  Charles Sahm, "What Explains the Success at Success Academy?," *Education Next*, Summer 2015, available at https://www.educationnext.org/what-explains-success-academy-charter-network/

50   Ibid.

51   "The Elementary School Curriculum," Success
     Academy, 2018-19, p. 15, available at https://www.
     successacademies.org/app/uploads/2018/05/es-
     curriculum-guide.pdf

52   Ibid.

53   "Setting a New Standard for Success in
     Education," The Brookings Institution/Carnegie
     Endowment, September 9, 2015, p. 4, available
     at https://www.brookings.edu/wp-content/
     uploads/2015/08/20150909_success_education_
     transcript.pdf

54   Ibid.

55   Ibid.

56   "Setting a New Standard for Success in
     Education," The Brookings Institution/Carnegie
     Endowment, September 9, 2015, p. 5, available
     at https://www.brookings.edu/wp-content/
     uploads/2015/08/20150909_success_education_
     transcript.pdf

57   Ibid.

58   Ibid.

59   Ibid, pp. 6-7.

60   Ibid, p. 7.

61   Ibid.

62   "Charles Sahm, "What Explains the Success at Success
     Academy?," *Education Next*, Summer 2015, available at
     https://www.educationnext.org/what-explains-success-
     academy-charter-network/

63   Ibid.

64   Ibid.

65   "Setting a New Standard for Success in
     Education," The Brookings Institution/Carnegie
     Endowment, September 9, 2015, p. 5, available
     at https://www.brookings.edu/wp-content/
     uploads/2015/08/20150909_success_education_
     transcript.pdf

66   Ibid.

67   Ibid.

68   "Charles Sahm, "What Explains the Success at Success
     Academy?," *Education Next*, Summer 2015, available at
     https://www.educationnext.org/what-explains-success-
     academy-charter-network/

69   "Setting a New Standard for Success in
     Education," The Brookings Institution/Carnegie
     Endowment, September 9, 2015, p. 5, available
     at https://www.brookings.edu/wp-content/
     uploads/2015/08/20150909_success_education_
     transcript.pdf

70   Eva Moskowitz, *The Education of Eva Moskowitz* (New
     York, NY: Harper Collins, 2017), p. 325.

71   Ibid, p. 344.

72   "Setting a New Standard for Success in
     Education," The Brookings Institution/Carnegie
     Endowment, September 9, 2015, p. 8, available
     at https://www.brookings.edu/wp-content/
     uploads/2015/08/20150909_success_education_
     transcript.pdf

# Chapter 7

1     See http://avondalemeadowsacademy.com/about-ama/academic-program/

2     "Spotlight on Indianapolis: Interview with School Director of Avondale Meadows Academy," Purpose Built Communities, January 16, 2015, available at https://purposebuiltcommunities.org/news-press/spotlight-indianapolis-interview-school-director-avondale-meadows-academy/

3     Ibid.

4     See http://avondalemeadowsacademy.com/about-ama/who-we-are/

5     See http://avondalemeadowsacademy.com/about-ama/academic-program/

6     Ibid.

7     Ibid.

8     "Spotlight on Indianapolis: Interview with School Director of Avondale Meadows Academy," Purpose Built Communities, January 16, 2015, available at https://purposebuiltcommunities.org/news-press/spotlight-indianapolis-interview-school-director-avondale-meadows-academy/

9     See http://avondalemeadowsacademy.com/about-ama/who-we-are/

10     See https://www.greatschools.org/indiana/indianapolis/3434-Avondale-Meadows-Academy-Formerly-The-Challenge-Foundation-Academy/

11     See https://www.dsstpublicschools.org/about-us

12   See https://www.dsstpublicschools.org/stapleton-high-school/college-success-curriculum-0

13   See https://broadfoundation.org/dsst-wins-the-2018-broad-prize-for-public-charter-schools/

# Conclusion

1   "Setting a New Standard for Success in Education," The Brookings Institution/Carnegie Endowment, September 9, 2015, p. 3, available at https://www.brookings.edu/wp-content/uploads/2015/08/20150909_success_education_transcript.pdf

2   Ibid, p. 8.

# ACKNOWLEDGEMENTS

Many people assisted in the preparation of this book. The author would like to thank Gary Larson and Brian Greenberg for their suggestions of innovative charter schools around the country. Cassandra Blazer coordinated the author's visits to Life Learning Academy. Laura Waters pointed the author to NYC Autism Charter School. Phillip Nanni and Keetha Mills provided important assistance for the section on Natomas Charter School. Margaret Fortune introduced the author to Cameron Curry and the Classical Academy. Christine Zanello was instrumental in facilitating the author's visits and interactions at Design Tech. Catherine Madden made the author's visits to Summit Shasta possible and provided key Summit documents. California Assemblyman Kevin Kiley alerted the author to the great work of John Adams Academy. Carlos Yniguez and Norman Gonzales made the author's visits to John Adams Academy possible, scheduled classroom tours, arranged interviews, and provided key school documents. Romeo Agbalog was instrumental in setting up the author's visits to Grimmway Academy Shasta.

The author would also like to thank Pacific Research Institute president and CEO Sally Pipes, PRI senior vice president Rowena Itchon and PRI communications director Tim Anaya for editing this book (any remaining errors or omissions are the sole responsibility of the author), graphic designer Dana Beigel, PRI vice president of development Ben Smithwick, and the other dedicated PRI staff who made this book possible. The author would also like to thank the Koret Foundation for the fellowship for the author.

The author of this book worked independently and his views and conclusions do not necessarily represent those of the board, supporters, and staff of PRI.

# ABOUT THE AUTHOR
## Lance Izumi

Lance Izumi is Senior Director of the Center for Education at the Pacific Research Institute, a public policy think tank based in San Francisco, Sacramento, and Pasadena, California. He is the author of numerous books, studies and articles on education policy issues, and served as co-executive producer of an award-winning PBS-broadcast documentary on underperforming middle-class public schools and co-executive producer, writer and narrator of a *New York Times*-posted short film on school choice.

From 2004 to 2015, he served as a member of the Board of Governors of the California Community Colleges, the largest system of higher education in the nation, and served two terms as president of the Board from 2008 to 2009.

In 2015, he was elected chair of the board of directors of the Foundation for California Community Colleges, the official non-profit that supports the community college system and the state Chancellor's Office.

He also served as a commissioner on the California Postsecondary Education Commission and as a member of the United States Civil Rights Commission's California Advisory Committee.

Previously, he served as chief speechwriter and director of writing and research for California Governor George Deukmejian and as speechwriter to United States Attorney General Edwin Meese III in President Ronald Reagan's administration.

Lance received his juris doctorate from the University of Southern California School of Law, his master of arts in political science from the University of California at Davis, and his bachelor of arts in economics and history from the University of California at Los Angeles.

# ABOUT
## Pacific Research Institute

The Pacific Research Institute (PRI) champions freedom, opportunity, and personal responsibility by advancing free-market policy solutions. It provides practical solutions for the policy issues that impact the daily lives of all Americans, and demonstrates why the free market is more effective than the government at providing the important results we all seek: good schools, quality health care, a clean environment, and a robust economy.

Founded in 1979 and based in San Francisco, PRI is a non-profit, non-partisan organization supported by private contributions. Its activities include publications, public events, media commentary, community leadership, legislative testimony, and academic outreach.

CPSIA information can be obtained
at www.ICGtesting.com
Printed in the USA
BVHW060933090720
583338BV00008B/472